Having Hope at Home

Having Hope at Home
A Comedy

David S. Craig

Playwrights Canada Press
Toronto • Canada

Playwrights Canada Press
The Canadian Drama Publisher
215 Spadina Avenue, Suite 230, Toronto, Ontario CANADA M5T 2C7
416-703-0013   fax 416-408-3402
orders@playwrightscanada.com • www.playwrightscanada.com

Playwrights Canada Press acknowledges the financial support of the Canadian taxpayer
through the Government of Canada Book Publishing Industry Development Programme
(BPIDP) for our publishing activities. We also acknowledge the Canadian and Ontario
taxpayers through the Canada Council for the Arts and the Ontario Arts Council.

The Canada Council for the Arts
Le Conseil des Arts du Canada

Front cover photo: "Keith Jones and his granddaughter, Maddison" courtesy of
Lighthouse Festival Theatre, Port Dover, Ontario. Back cover photo by Terry Manzo,
Stratford. l to r: Caroline Gillis, Ross Manson, Shawn Mathieson, Mary Krohnert, Jerry
Franken, Michelle Fisk.
Production editing/cover design: JLArt

Library and Archives Canada Cataloguing in Publication

Craig, David S. (David Stewart)
     Having hope at home : a comedy / David S. Craig.

A play.
ISBN 0-88754-758-3

     I. Title.

PS8555.R265H39 2005   C812'.54   C2005-902623-5

First edition: May 2005.
Printed and bound by Printco at Scarborough, Canada.

To Robin with Love

Introduction

Reading the first draft of *Having Hope at Home*, I immediately fell in love with its brash approach to the family dynamic. Its characters are familiar, drawn from classical comic prototypes. The wisecracking old grampa, an uptight, tyrannical father and his ultra conservative wife— the Dionysian, exotic son-in-law and, at the centre of the piece, the beleaguered daughter who is determined to put the world right. This play wears the very essence of comedy on its sleeve—the world is out of order. By the end of the play, despite endless misunderstandings, order is restored.

David's writing is irresistible. The time-honoured blend of celebration and strife within a squabbling family is simultaneously universal and specific to our place and time. We all struggle at some point to finally claim our lives as adults—but it happens at a very different pace for everyone. *Having Hope at Home* reminds us that the choices we make during these times have a profound effect on our loved ones. It also reminds us that we must face the choices that our children will one day make. The fact that David makes us laugh while offering these reminders makes the journey that much sweeter.

The opening night of the Blyth Festival premiere was rife with laughter so intense that it threatened to derail the performance on a few occasions. Word of mouth worked its magic and tickets went like wildfire. But more importantly, it quickly received the most elusive and important vote of confidence in Canadian theatre: subsequent productions with professional companies. This is a script that delights and endures. Bravo, David.

—Eric Coates, Artistic Director, Blyth Festival

Playwright's Notes—*Having Hope at Home*

Some of us get married, some of us have children but all of us, through no fault of our own, have families. You either love them, put up with them or move to Vancouver. In my lifetime, I have seen the ties of family weaken as we, myself included, have gone off to seek our individual goals of glory and personal fulfillment. I'm not sure we're better off. In fact I'm almost certain humans are pack animals and our separation from the tribe, despite the potent freedom it provides, is causing us a great deal of anxiety. My sense is that reconciliation, with ourselves, our families, our communities and our world, is the challenge of our age. Anyone who tells me that our lives can devolve into depression, suicide, divorce, murder, war, addiction and chaos is telling me a story I already know. 9/11 etched that tale on my brain like acid on a copper plate. The story I am longing to hear must show people creeping back from isolation towards the vulnerability of community. I want to see them succeed (comedy) or fail trying (tragedy). That is the theme of this play and the argument behind its happy ending. No one will leave the theatre fooled into thinking that life is always like that, but I propose that the tenuous moment of peace that this family discovers is well earned and much appreciated. It gives hope and a trail of stones through the forest.

—DSC

Acknowledgements

My thanks to Janet Amos who commissioned the play, Robert More who developed it and Eric Coates who ultimately produced and directed the premiere. Thanks also go to Dawn King, our first midwife. It was her story, about a mother whose labour stopped upon the untimely and judgmental arrival of her parents, that got the whole thing started. Thanks to Bridget Lynch, our second midwife, who read the script and commented on all things medical. Thanks to the Italian playwright Eduardo de Fillipo. It would amaze him to know that his play *Saturday, Sunday, Monday* in an English production at the Old Vic starring Laurence Olivier would inspire a young Canadian playwright to create a different but parallel family that would delight an audience in Ontario's Huron County, but that's what happened. And finally thanks to Russell Munro who was the inspiration for Russell Bingham. He really did duct tape his rheumy hand to the chainsaw and he really did take heart attack pills every day. If there's a Canadian Tire catalogue in heaven, Mr. Munro will be reading it. *Merci tous!*

Having Hope at Home premiered at the Blyth Festival, Ontario, in August 2003 with the following company:

Carolyn	Mary Krohnert
Russell	Jerry Franken
Michel	Shawn Mathieson
Jane	Michelle Fisk
Bill	Ross Manson
Dawn	Caroline Gillis

Eric Coates, Artistic Director

Director: Eric Coates
Set and Costume Design: Andjelija Djuric
Lighting Design: Renée Brode
Stage Manager: Kate Macdonnell
Assistant Stage Manager: Sarah Dalgleish

Having Hope at Home was originally commissioned by the Blyth Festival (Janet Amos, Artistic Director) and subsequently developed by the Lighthouse Theatre, Port Dover (Robert More, Artistic Director).

Characters

Carolyn (Caro) Bingham
Russell (Gramps) Bingham, Carolyn's grandfather
Michel (Mish) Charbonneau, Carolyn's husband
William (Bill) Bingham, Carolyn's father
Jane Bingham, Carolyn's mother
Dawn Shaw, Carolyn's midwife

Time and Place

Act I: The present.   Act II: A few minutes later.

The action takes place on a cold winter night in the kitchen of Russell Bingham's old farmhouse. This is its last winter. The foundation of "the new house" (across the road) has been poured, construction will begin in the spring and they (Russell, his granddaughter Carolyn, her husband Michel and their new baby) will move in after Labour Day if they can afford it. But that is all in the future. For the moment they are in the old, drafty, un-renovated house. In fact, the farmhouse is so poorly insulated, they have stopped heating unused rooms, including the living room and most of the second floor.

Their living space consists of a large farm kitchen. Insulation has been stuffed into cracks and holes. Wallpaper is peeling. Kitchen cabinets are broken or eccentrically repaired. Yet, there are clear signs of imagination and care. There are flowers, stencils, some lovely old pine pieces (stripped and restored), photos of ancestors, books and paintings that indicate care, not decay. To the critical eye, it looks like a ruin but to the forgiving eye, it speaks of home.

The layout of the kitchen is as follows: upstage right, moving left, is the back door, which leads to the mudroom and the yard, the telephone (with a long cable), the fridge, a kitchen counter (including a sink facing windows), the oven and the door into the rest of the house. From centre stage right, moving left, is the wood stove, a dining room table which, as the curtain opens, is set for dinner (a dinner which, should a concerned stage manager be reading these lines, is served but never eaten) and the door leading to Carolyn and Michel's main floor bedroom. Downstage right, moving left, is the door to the bathroom, Russell's chair, a sofa (with a cedar chest in front acting as a coffee table) and the trapdoor[1] to the basement. On the stage left apron is Russell's wood pile.

[1] Where a trap is not feasible, a vertical door would also work.

Having Hope at Home

ACT I

Scene One – Before

Lights up. A hand appears from behind the sofa. Another hand. CAROLYN's head appears.

CAROLYN   *(amazed)* Oh. My. Gosh. *(calling)* Mish...? Gramps...?

She stands. She is nine months pregnant, and she has been washing the floor. She goes to the telephone.

Ohmigosh, ohmigosh, ohmigosh.

She dials.

Dawn it's me. Something's happening. I've been having little pinges all day but just now I had the mother of all cramps. It was like an alien was inside my body ripping open the floor of my uterus. How do I stop it? //[2] Yes honey, I would like to speak to your mummy. // Can you put the movie on "pause"? // Thank you. *(to herself)* Please, baby, not now, not now. *(calling)* Mish! *(into the receiver)* Dawn? Ohmigosh, I just gave all my symptoms to your six-year-old. Tell her I was describing a movie. A horror movie. It may not be too far from the truth. // No, there's nothing wrong. But there is something happening. I think I just had my first contraction. // Five seconds. // Intense but bearable. // No, I forgot to breathe completely. Except when I was yelling. // No, it's not perfect. In fifteen minutes my parents will be arriving for dinner.

RUSSELL comes scurrying in the back door.

---

[2] // indicates that the character is listening to someone speak on the telephone.

	Grampa, where have you been?
RUSSELL	Well…
CAROLYN	You're supposed to be helping me get ready.
RUSSELL	Oh…?
CAROLYN	Have you fixed the toilet?
RUSSELL	Uh…
CAROLYN	Have you brought in the firewood?
RUSSELL	*(remembering he hasn't)* Oh yes…
CAROLYN	They're going to be here any minute.
RUSSELL	Right you are.

RUSSELL exits outside. CAROLYN moves to the sofa.

CAROLYN   Listen, I gotta go. I just wanted you to know things were happening so you could… // *(urgent)* No, you can't come over. // My parents don't know about you. // I can't cancel. That's what they expect me to do. That's why I'm having the dinner. To prove I can do something without cancelling. Besides they're already on the way and my mother made a point of saying that my father "wasn't wearing his pager." My father doesn't have a shower without his pager so it's a really big deal. // To you it's "just a dinner." To me it's a high-level peace summit between two warring nations. // I wish I was exaggerating. Months of negotiations have led to this dinner, because tonight, for the first time in my life, I am going to do something stunningly symbolic. I am going to serve dinner to my parents. Dinner in my house, under my roof, by my rules and they will suddenly see that I am a fully adult human being, capable of making fully adult decisions. And when the clouds part and they see the shining adultness of my being they will sue for peace, get off my back and become the gentle, doting grandparents I want them to be. That's why I can't cancel the dinner. That and the small fact that my father is the Head of Gynaecology at City Hospital. If he arrives and finds me having a home birth, with a midwife, he'll never talk to me again. //

Why do you need his pulse? // Okay, okay, but let's make it quick. I have to peel the carrots. I'll count and you time it.

> CAROLYN *puts on a stethoscope and holds it to her belly.*

Hold on. I just gotta find the little dickens.... Oh! There he is. Ready? One, two, three... (*continues*)

> RUSSELL *enters. He's in a panic. He opens the trapdoor to the basement and disappears.*

MICHEL   (*off*) Russell!!!

> MICHEL *enters. He is a gorgeous, raven-haired man, slightly shorter than* CAROLYN *but perfectly proportioned. He is furious. He speaks with a French-Canadian accent.*

Where is he?

CAROLYN   (*to* MICHEL) Boots! (*to* DAWN) Ten, eleven, twelve... (*continues*)

MICHEL   (*looking down into the basement*) Is he down there? Are you down there? I hope so, because I'm going to pass down there and break every bone in your body.

CAROLYN   Mish! Get changed. Nineteen, twenty...

MICHEL   Russell was in the barn.

CAROLYN   Who cares. My parents are coming. Twenty-three, twenty-four, twenty-five...

MICHEL   He was in the milk room.

CAROLYN   Did he pump the milk down the drain?

MICHEL   No.

CAROLYN   Did he pump the milk back into the cows?

MICHEL   He took the milker apart. It's in pieces all over the floor.

CAROLYN   Then put a bigger lock on the door. I've got more important things on my mind. (*to* DAWN) Thirty-seven, thirty-eight, thirty-nine.... Is that enough?

MICHEL	*(instantly solicitous)* Is the baby coming?
CAROLYN	*(listening to DAWN)* Yes.
MICHEL	Really?
CAROLYN	*(listening to DAWN)* Of course.
MICHEL	*(sinking to his knees in rapture)* The baby is coming!
CAROLYN	*(to MICHEL)* What? No. The baby is not coming. My parents are coming. And you promised to help. So please shave your face, put on a clean shirt—NOT the cowboy shirt—and don't worry about the cows, okay?
MICHEL	Okay.
CAROLYN	Now go.
MICHEL	Okay.
CAROLYN	And find Grampa.
MICHEL	That's just what I was going to…
CAROLYN	*(to DAWN)* Sorry. Yes, that was Michel. // Yeah, he's pretty excited. So what was the baby's pulse? // Well, there you go. We've got lots of time.

> *MICHEL goes down the stairs to the basement.*
> *RUSSELL emerges from the basement, shuts the door*
> *and stands on it.*

	Grampa?
RUSSELL	Yeah.
CAROLYN	Where'd Michel go?
RUSSELL	I think he's in the barn.
MICHEL	*(off, tries to open the door)* Hey!
RUSSELL	Well look at that, he's in the basement.
MICHEL	*(off, pounding)* Get off!
RUSSELL	You know, Carolyn, there's just no respect for the elderly these days, no reverence for the wisdom of years.
MICHEL	*(off)* Get off the door right now!!!!!

CAROLYN	*(gently)* Grampa…
RUSSELL	Okay, I'll let him out, but you hide the shotgun.

RUSSELL steps away from the door and heads for the porch. MICHEL is right behind him. RUSSELL cuts downstage and across in front of the sofa.

MICHEL	Come back here…
RUSSELL	I didn't do anything…
CAROLYN	Michel…
MICHEL	I told you.
RUSSELL	Stay back!
MICHEL	Don't go…
RUSSELL	He's going to kill me.
MICHEL	Into the milk room!
RUSSELL	Help!
CAROLYN	Michel!

The game stops. CAROLYN is between them.

Do I have to deal with this right now?

MICHEL	I told him. Don't touch. Does he listen? No. He's deaf in the head.
RUSSELL	I was helping out. What's wrong with that?
CAROLYN	He was just helping out.
RUSSELL	It's my farm.
MICHEL	And it's my equipment and I don't want him touching it.
CAROLYN	Why not?
MICHEL	He's not trained.
RUSSELL	Hah! He thinks I'm useless. The Frenchman's calling me useless.
MICHEL	You're not useless. You're just useless to me.

CAROLYN	He doesn't mean that Grampa.
RUSSELL	Yes he does. I've got a bad heart and rheumy hands and he thinks I'm useless when I can do more work than all the frogs in China.
MICHEL	You mean do more damage.
	CAROLYN begins to slowly double over with a contraction.
RUSSELL	Don't talk to me, froggy. You just take your froggy legs and swim back down the St. Lawrence where you belong.
MICHEL	Maybe I will, you *maudit* Anglo racist cow dog. You would freeze to death without me. You can't even light a match without me.
CAROLYN	Stop.
MICHEL	Caro?
CAROLYN	Oh don't worry about me. I'm just the pregnant mother of your unborn child. What am I compared to your beloved cows?
MICHEL	What's wrong?
RUSSELL	*(to MICHEL)* Baby.
MICHEL	Are you in labour?
RUSSELL	She is. Believe me. When they get mouthy like that, you know.
CAROLYN	You want to live another second? *(gasps)* Dawn, ohmigosh, are you still there? // Oh, everything's fine. I'll give you a call in the morning. *(to MICHEL)* Would you hang up the phone? *(beat)* Please. *(beat)* Mish.
MICHEL	Are you in labour?
CAROLYN	No. If I was in labour, I'd be talking to your mother.
MICHEL	But you just had a contraction.
CAROLYN	That was gas.
MICHEL	It was a contraction.

CAROLYN	How would you know?
MICHEL	*(whisper)* Because if it was gas, you wouldn't be talking to the midwife.
CAROLYN	Okay, I had, what might be called a contraction. The first contraction of my first labour. It could last for hours, days. My parents are arriving any minute.
RUSSELL	And if there's an emergency, I can handle it. I've played midwife to hundreds of cows. You just reach in, grab the back hoof and pull them out. You should see the look of gratitude on the cow's face. 'Course it's slippery work. I've been known to drop some of them on their heads.
MICHEL	*(taking the telephone)* Dawn? It's me. Can you come over right now?
CAROLYN	Noooooooooo!
RUSSELL	Now, sweetie, you can't reschedule a baby.
CAROLYN	Don't you sweetie me.
RUSSELL	Yes ma'am.
MICHEL	Great. *(hangs up)* She's on her way.
CAROLYN	Why are you guys ignoring what I want? I'm not worried about having a baby. I could have a baby in a barn, in a field, on a roller coaster. What I can't do, without your help, is have a pleasant dinner with my parents.
MICHEL	Carolyn.
CAROLYN	What?
MICHEL	Come here.
CAROLYN	No.
MICHEL	Okay. I'm coming over there.
	MICHEL joyfully dances towards CAROLYN.
CAROLYN	Mish? Mish what are you doing?
MICHEL	The baby is coming.

He falls to his knees and kisses CAROLYN's belly.

RUSSELL   There he goes being emotional.

CAROLYN   *(loving it)* Mish… Mish stop. Stop. Stop!

MICHEL   Is there anything I can do?

CAROLYN   Anything you can…. What is it about the male personality that allows you both to stand in the middle of a million things to do and say with total innocence, "is there anything I can do?!"

MICHEL   I'll make you a cup of tea.

CAROLYN   No! Mish. Gramps. I'm going to cry. Because you guys are totally ignoring what I want. My parents, your in-laws, your son and daughter-in-law are coming to dinner. I've asked you to fix the toilet. I've asked you to put on a clean shirt. I've asked you to help me the way I help you every day of the year. No. Not every day, every damn day. Every double damn, double day, double double damn… *(She weeps.)* What's happening?

RUSSELL   *(whispering)* Hormones.

CAROLYN   You had to say that didn't you?

RUSSELL   I knew you'd want to know.

MICHEL   *(tentatively)* What do you want done first?

CAROLYN   *(She takes a deep breath.)* Cut the carrots.

RUSSELL   You stay with her. I'll cut the carrots.

CAROLYN   You can't hold a knife.

RUSSELL   I can manage.

CAROLYN   You can barely hold a fork.

RUSSELL   Do you think I'm useless too?

CAROLYN   Of course not. If you could cut the carrots it would be a big help.

             CAROLYN and MICHEL move into bedroom. CAROLYN tries to find her make-up. MICHEL tries to find a clean shirt.

MICHEL	What are you doing?
CAROLYN	I have to put on some lipstick.
MICHEL	Why?
CAROLYN	It's for my mother. She doesn't go to the grocery store without lipstick.
MICHEL	So tonight you will "make-up" with your mother.
CAROLYN	I hope so. She'll probably arrive with something expensive. Something in a Birks Box that was actually bought at Birks. What I need is a new carburetor for the rototiller but she'll bring a sterling silver cake cutter.
MICHEL	At least she tries.
CAROLYN	Unlike my Father. Last night I dreamt I'd just given birth to a beautiful baby boy. There I was, alone with the baby, with you and Gramps and a few thousand other people cheering and waving flags, and then suddenly I was alone in a dark room, with my father pointing a bright light at me saying, "put the baby back, Carolyn, you've done it wrong." And I said, "I can't put it back. It's breathing," and he said, "Do what I say. I'm a doctor."
MICHEL	It's just a dream.
CAROLYN	Or an omen.
MICHEL	We're not doing open heart surgery. We're having a baby. With a midwife. After careful thought and months of preparation.
CAROLYN	And it's going to be great, right?
MICHEL	It's going to be perfect.
	RUSSELL has been struggling to hold a carrot and the knife. At this point they drop to the ground.
CAROLYN	Grampa?
RUSSELL	Yeah.
CAROLYN	You okay?

RUSSELL	Oh yeah.
CAROLYN	I think he's nervous too.
MICHEL	You worry too much about your parents. I have parents, crazy parents, but I don't worry about them.
CAROLYN	Your parents are different. They laugh.
MICHEL	And fight.
CAROLYN	I love the way they fight.
MICHEL	You'd like it less if you knew what they were saying.

> *RUSSELL, in frustration, begins to rapidly bite pieces of carrot and spit them into the pot. It makes a noise.*

CAROLYN	Grampa?
RUSSELL	Yeah?
CAROLYN	How's it going?
RUSSELL	Oh I'm doing fine now.

> *He takes the pot and exits.*

CAROLYN	When my parents fight, they don't yell. That would be losing control. They just disapprove, and I am their Great Disappointment.
MICHEL	Why? Because you live here? With the space and the stars and the quiet.
CAROLYN	And you. I know. I love this life. So why do I feel like a failure?
MICHEL	Caro—if your parents can't see what a great life you have, they are as blind as bats.
CAROLYN	But what if I have another contraction...
MICHEL	Why do we need to hide it?
CAROLYN	Because my dad is the Head of Gynaecology and my mother is the Head of Fundraising for Gynaecology. They've spent their lives putting pregnant women into hospitals.

MICHEL	So? We don't need a hospital.
CAROLYN	I can't tell them that.
MICHEL	Why not?
CAROLYN	Because it will upset them. And tonight I don't want anyone upset.

They re-enter the kitchen.

MICHEL	So we have to lie.
CAROLYN	Absolutely. We have to give them something they understand. A formal, sit-down dinner.
MICHEL	Why should I lie about something I'm proud of.
CAROLYN	Please. Mish. All I need is a few hours. Just a few hours.
MICHEL	I am being manipulated.
CAROLYN	Shut up and say okay.
MICHEL	Okay.
CAROLYN	Thank you.

They kiss. RUSSELL enters with the pot and sees them.

RUSSELL	Oh my. The bull's in with the cows.
MICHEL	In case you haven't noticed, the bull got in with the cows nine months ago.
RUSSELL	I know. The walls aren't that thick.
CAROLYN	Grampa!
RUSSELL	Carrots are done.
CAROLYN	They're beautiful.
RUSSELL	I did 'em fancy.
CAROLYN	Now go put on your tie. *(to MICHEL)* And you change your shirt. And not the cowboy shirt. I want everything to be perfect.

MICHEL exits.

Because as soon as they walk in here, they will be judging every move we make.

RUSSELL is struggling with his tie.

Can I help?

RUSSELL	Damn thing. My fingers got no purchase anymore. The right's got a bit but the left. *(He glares at his left hand.)* Arrr… the left…
CAROLYN	Are you talking about your hand or your politics?
RUSSELL	Is the rhubarb pie ready to go?
CAROLYN	All ready.
RUSSELL	And you used the right recipe?
CAROLYN	Lorna Bingham's Red Ribbon.
RUSSELL	And the turkey?
CAROLYN	In the oven.
RUSSELL	Twenty minutes to the pound?
CAROLYN	It's all timed, Grampa. They'll walk in the door, have a drink and dinner will float effortlessly from the kitchen to the table.
RUSSELL	Not like your meatloaf.

CAROLYN has a contraction which slowly bends her over. She doesn't notice that she is still holding onto RUSSELL's tie and is dragging him down with her.

CAROLYN	No.
RUSSELL	I still have that meatloaf.
CAROLYN	You do?
RUSSELL	It's under the wheel of my tractor to keep it from rolling.
CAROLYN	That's… great.

MICHEL enters doing up his cowboy shirt and sees each of them bent over.

MICHEL	Caro?

CAROLYN	I'm fine
RUSSELL	She's got my tie.
MICHEL	Carolyn, let go.
CAROLYN	*(releasing it)* Sorry.
RUSSELL	I'd say that baby's headed for the hopper.
CAROLYN	No it's not.
MICHEL	How did it feel?
CAROLYN	Just a twinge.
MICHEL	Stronger than before?
CAROLYN	Maybe a little.
RUSSELL	Could come fast. My Lorna had 'em fast.
CAROLYN	We're not calling off this dinner.
MICHEL	Are you going to give birth between courses?
CAROLYN	If I have to.
RUSSELL	I don't think she had 'em that fast.
MICHEL	And how are we going to explain Dawn?
CAROLYN	I'm not the one who told her to come.
RUSSELL	We could say she's my girlfriend. *(beat)* Why not?
MICHEL	Let's hide her in the barn.
RUSSELL	Good idea, I'll give her a tour.
CAROLYN & MICHEL	You're staying here.

A car honks. They freeze. They rush to the window.

RUSSELL	It's them.

CAROLYN creates a receiving line, then changes it. Tension.

CAROLYN	Did you fix the toilet?
RUSSELL	No.

CAROLYN	Why are you wearing a cowboy shirt?
MICHEL	You told me to.
	Tension.
CAROLYN	Don't forget. My dad likes Scotch and my mum likes wine.
RUSSELL	Let me serve the drinks.
CAROLYN	No. You're on medication.
RUSSELL	Uh-huh.
CAROLYN	And no running off.
RUSSELL	Uh-huh. *(beat)* Why are we doing this?
CAROLYN	Shhh.
RUSSELL	I'd prefer to stick pins in my blisters.
CAROLYN	Try to make your son feel welcome.
RUSSELL	Uh-huh.
CAROLYN	'Cause everyone is going to have a really nice time.
MICHEL	Here they come.
	RUSSELL bolts for the door to the rest of the house.
CAROLYN	Grampa!
RUSSELL	I forgot something.
MICHEL	Coward.
	Before she can protest there's a knock on the door. MICHEL opens it.

Scene Two – The Guests Arrive

ALL	Hello! We're here!
CAROLYN	Welcome.

JANE	Carolyn.
CAROLYN	*(They embrace.)* Hi Mum.
BILL	Good to see you, Michael.
MICHEL	Let me take your coats.
JANE	Oh honey, look at you. I can't believe it. You're having a baby.
CAROLYN	Looks like it.
JANE	Here's your father.
BILL	Hello Carolyn.
CAROLYN	Hi Dad.
BILL	You look well.
CAROLYN	I feel great.
BILL	Looks like a big one.
JANE	The Binghams always have big babies. I know. I had three of them.
CAROLYN	Michel's family has big babies too.
JANE	Really?
MICHEL	Monsters.

They look at MICHEL.

BILL	Really. *(back to CAROLYN)* When are you due?
CAROLYN	Pretty soon.
BILL	You're carrying very low. How are you presenting?
JANE	Bill.
BILL	Sorry. Why am I sorry?
JANE	You're off duty.
BILL	I was just saying her labour could come earlier than she thinks.
JANE	Carolyn knows when she's due.

BILL	So you say, but I can't count the number of women who come through my office who can't calculate forty weeks. Simple math and they can't add it up.
CAROLYN	I can count to forty, Dad.
JANE	Of course you can.

Awkward silence.

MICHEL	Why don't you come in and sit down.
JANE	Thank you, Michel.
BILL	Where's Dad?
CAROLYN	He just went to get something.
JANE	Carolyn. You look gorgeous.
CAROLYN	Me? Really? I feel so big.
JANE	Your complexion is beautiful and your hair…
CAROLYN	I let it grow.
JANE	It suits you.
CAROLYN	I thought you'd hate it.
JANE	I love it. And your lipstick. What colour is that?
CAROLYN	Uh. Red.
JANE	It's lovely.
CAROLYN	Thanks Mum.
JANE	Well… I can't believe it's been so long.
CAROLYN	Neither can I.
JANE	Three years.
CAROLYN	We've been so busy.
JANE	Oh you have. With the farm and looking after Russell…
CAROLYN	I've wanted you to come.
BILL	All we needed was an invitation.
JANE	And we got one and here we are.

Awkward silence.

CAROLYN	I was hoping I could entertain you in the new house.
JANE	How's it coming?
CAROLYN	We've poured the foundation.
JANE	That's wonderful.
BILL	I was expecting to see some walls and a roof.
CAROLYN	We had to make some improvements to the milk room. That's why we fixed up over here.
JANE	My... it's...
CAROLYN	Cozy?
JANE	Yes.
CAROLYN	We've added a lot of insulation.
BILL	I can see that.
JANE	I didn't know insulation was so colourful.

RUSSELL enters.

CAROLYN	Here's Grampa.
BILL	Hi Dad.
RUSSELL	Hello.

They wait for the men to say more. They don't.

CAROLYN	Sit down Grampa.
JANE	Maybe we'd be more comfortable sitting in the living room?
CAROLYN	We don't use the living room.
JANE	Oh?
CAROLYN	It's too hard to heat.
RUSSELL	And the floor's rotten.
JANE	Rotten?
RUSSELL	Step in the wrong place and you'll land smack in the basement.

JANE	Well we don't want that.
CAROLYN	That's why we like it in here.
JANE	Where it's cozy.
CAROLYN	Yes.
JANE	Well then…

They sit in silence.

MICHEL	Bill. Would you like a Scotch?
BILL	Sure. One finger.
MICHEL	Jane.
JANE	Nothing for me, thank you. Carolyn. I brought you an early housewarming present.
CAROLYN	You didn't need to do that.
JANE	I wanted to. I've missed seeing you open your presents at Christmas. You always go to Michel's family.
CAROLYN	*(looking at MICHEL)* Well… the last few years, there's always been something going on in Quebec… a wedding or a funeral.
BILL	At Christmas?
MICHEL	Or a baptism or a confirmation.
CAROLYN	Michel has such a big family.
RUSSELL	Big and religious.
CAROLYN	Grampa.
JANE	Maybe next year you could come to us.
CAROLYN	Oh?
JANE	With the baby.
CAROLYN	Well…
MICHEL	We'll decide on that in the Fall.

Silence.

JANE	*(indicating the present)* Aren't you going to open it?

CAROLYN	Sure. Oh wow. A Birks box.
	She removes a china figurine.
	Oh Mum. It's beautiful.
JANE	Turn it over.
CAROLYN	Royal Doulton.
BILL	Only the best.
JANE	Your father thinks I'm a broken record but I felt sure you'd like this one.
CAROLYN	Look Mish. It's a mother and baby.
JANE	Do you have a place to display it?
CAROLYN	Display it?
JANE	I think nice things should be displayed.
RUSSELL	You mean like a rifle?
CAROLYN	I dunno. Grampa and Mish crash around a lot.
JANE	There must be some place nice where you can put it.
CAROLYN	I know. The toaster oven.
JANE	The toaster oven?
CAROLYN	It's out of the way and I'd see it every morning.
JANE	The toaster oven would be wonderful. Let's put it there right now.
CAROLYN	*(this means getting up)* Uh… okay.
JANE	Do you need any help?
CAROLYN	No. No. I'm fine.
	They move upstage together. MICHEL brings out the drinks. RUSSELL gets milk.
MICHEL	Drinks.
BILL	Thanks Michael. You call that one finger?
MICHEL	Sure. *(showing a vertical finger)* One finger.
BILL	How's your heart doing, Dad?

RUSSELL	Fine.
BILL	And your arthritis?
RUSSELL	Fine.
BILL	Are you still cutting wood?
RUSSELL	Some.
BILL	You're not still using a chainsaw, are you?
RUSSELL	No, I got some trained beavers. Of course I use a chainsaw.
BILL	I'm amazed you can still pick it up.
RUSSELL	It's simple. I duct tape my left hand to the handle and my right hand to the pull cord. These two fingers still work good so I use them on the throttle.
BILL	And one day you'll cut your leg off.
RUSSELL	Then I'll duct-tape it back on.

> *MICHEL laughs. BILL turns and looks at him. MICHEL stops.*

BILL	You shouldn't be using power tools at all.
RUSSELL	Out with the old, eh?
BILL	You've worked your whole life.
RUSSELL	I know. That's why I can't quit.
BILL	You deserve a rest.
RUSSELL	How can you rest if you don't work?
BILL	Dad, it's dangerous. Why not let Michael run the chainsaw.
RUSSELL	He's got enough work. You should see the milk room. You could eat off the floor of that milk room. After dinner, I'll show you.
MICHEL	No you won't. I'll show him.
BILL	No thanks. I've seen enough of milk rooms to last me a lifetime.

RUSSELL	It's changed since you were there.
BILL	It hasn't changed enough.
RUSSELL	You just didn't like work. You should see the Frenchman out there. He knows how to work.
BILL	I don't think it was the work. I think it was the company.
RUSSELL	Hah!

JANE and CAROLYN return.

JANE	You men getting along?

There is an embarrassed silence.

RUSSELL	I'll get some firewood.
CAROLYN	We've got enough Grampa.
RUSSELL	This is just birch. For the chill in this room you need ironwood.

He exits. The women sit down.

CAROLYN	Grampa uses a different kind of wood for every occasion. He's a real connoisseur.
BILL	You heat the whole house with this little stove?
CAROLYN	Uh-huh. Some mornings, I have to break the ice in the toilet but mostly it burns all night.
JANE	Speaking of connoisseurs, your father has some news.
CAROLYN	What is it, Dad?
BILL	It's nothing.
JANE	Yes it is. He's put a wine cellar in the basement.
CAROLYN	Wow. What's it like?
BILL	Climate controlled. Look, Carolyn, I wish you wouldn't let Dad carry wood.
CAROLYN	He likes it.
BILL	His heart could give out any minute.
CAROLYN	He doesn't care about that.

2

24 David S. Craig

BILL   Well, I do and you should.

CAROLYN   Dad. Every day Grampa gets up, puts on his boots and
              walks over to the barn. Then he realizes he doesn't
              have to be in the barn.

MICHEL   That I won't let him in the barn...

CAROLYN   And he gets depressed.

JANE   Isn't there a programme in town for seniors?

MICHEL   Yes. It's called the Legion.

CAROLYN   But he's not supposed to drink and he can't hold cards.

JANE   But surely he's got some hobbies. When my father
              retired he liked to play the stock market.

CAROLYN   Grampa likes to play with a front end loader.

BILL   I'm just saying, as a doctor, he needs to slow down.

CAROLYN   He's your father. You try telling him.

BILL   I will.

JANE   Well then that's settled.

              *JANE moves upstage to the dining room table, BILL
              to the door. Unnoticed, CAROLYN begins a long,
              strong contraction while digging her nails into
              MICHEL's knee.*

              Carolyn, is that Gramma Bingham's china on the table?

CAROLYN   Yup.

JANE   I noticed it as soon as I walked in the door. I love
              old floral patterns. But I couldn't help thinking what
              a shame you don't have any sterling to go with it.

CAROLYN   Mum. I don't need silver cutlery.

JANE   But darling, you already have some.

CAROLYN   I do?

JANE   Don't you remember? My mother always gave you
              a piece on your birthday. "For your trousseau," she
              said. And you think *I'm* traditional. I took a look and

do you know there must be at least six place settings, two serving bowls and a candelabra. Now, I know you and Michel don't have any wedding plans—you don't do you?

CAROLYN   Nope.

JANE   So I was thinking, why keep them locked up? Why not give them to you now? So you can use them.

               JANE sees CAROLYN cramped over looking at the floor.

               Carolyn? What's wrong?

CAROLYN   Nothing. I just noticed there's no cranberry sauce on the table.

               JANE and BILL slowly look behind them at the dining table.

JANE   You're right.

CAROLYN   Can't have turkey without cranberry sauce.

               She stands up. She's a little spaced.

JANE   Let me get it.

CAROLYN   No, no. You stay there. It's no trouble at all. I just have to go *(to MICHEL)* to the basement.

JANE   *(worried)* Oh dear. Let Michel get it.

CAROLYN   I can't. He won't know the right jar. I've got the perfect one all picked out.

JANE   Bill, stop her.

CAROLYN   It's okay. I'm up and down these stairs every day. Mish will help me. I'll be right back. Drink up.

               CAROLYN and MICHEL exit into the basement.

BILL   Wonderful. You arrive for dinner, you're handed a jug of Scotch and then everyone disappears.

JANE   Bill. I can't believe Carolyn's living like this.

BILL   Like what?

JANE	Look around! There's insulation sticking out of all the walls.
BILL	They like it like that. It's cozy.
JANE	This is not cozy. This is the face of poverty.
BILL	Now hold on. They may be living poor but I bet they've got two hundred thousand tied up in that milk room.
JANE	Borrowed. Every penny of it.
BILL	A lot of decent people have bank loans, ourselves included.
JANE	Yes. To buy a wine cellar.
BILL	Why shouldn't I have a wine cellar?
JANE	Because our daughter is living in a dump.
BILL	Look. We gave that girl everything. And what did she do? Quit. Lessons, jobs, education, opportunities another kid would die for, that I would have died for, and she quit. What am I supposed to do?
JANE	Build her a house.
BILL	Oh c'mon.
JANE	They've built a foundation. What would it cost to finish it?
BILL	I wouldn't offer it and she wouldn't accept it.
JANE	How do you know?
BILL	She wants to be independent. She wants Christmas in Quebec.
JANE	She's just being proud.
BILL	Ha! Look around. Do you see pride here? No. What you see is stubbornness.
JANE	And where did she get that from?
BILL	My father.
JANE	Oh Bill.

BILL	All right. She got it from me. And it's a good thing too. Running a family farm will require all the stubbornness she can get.
JANE	Bill, she's our daughter. And she's going to have our grandchild. Our only grandchild.
BILL	What about Joyce? What about Troy?
JANE	Joyce is married to her job and Troy... Troy isn't going to marry anyone.
BILL	He might... now that they've changed the law.
JANE	Bill, face it. Carolyn is our only hope. And there is hope. This dinner is a peace offering. She wants to come home.
BILL	Like the prodigal son.
JANE	Yes.
BILL	She'll drive us crazy. She's always driven us crazy.
JANE	She might not. She's an adult now. We have to accept her as an adult.
BILL	So you think I should open my forgiving arms and kill the fatted calf.
JANE	You don't have to kill anything. Just build her a decent place to live.
BILL	She drops out of university and I build her a house.
JANE	Because you love her. That's what the Bible is trying to show us.
BILL	I never liked that parable. I always thought the prodigal son should have been cut off. Would have done him a world of good. I liked the other brother. He was a worker.
JANE	I'll pay for it myself.
BILL	How?
JANE	I'll cash in my RRSP.
BILL	No you won't.

JANE	Are we going to fight over this? I will not have my daughter living in a dump.
BILL	But you're treating her like a child.
JANE	I'm not the one with a wine cellar.
BILL	And I'm not the one who brags about it to everyone! Look. Carolyn has made her bed and now she has to lie in it. And with that wood fire, I bet it's a damn frosty bed in the morning.

RUSSELL enters with a huge stack of firewood.

Here. Dad. Let me give you a hand.

RUSSELL	I can manage. *(He drops the wood into the wood box.)* I've been managing for quite a while.

RUSSELL stands out of breath.

JANE	Russell, may I use the washroom?
RUSSELL	Sure.

JANE crosses towards SL door.

Oh, uh…. You'll need to pull the duck.

JANE	The duck?
RUSSELL	Yeah. When you go in, you'll see a duck floating in the tank. Grab it hard. Grab it 'till it squeaks.
JANE	Grab the duck.
RUSSELL	Yeah. And pull.
JANE	Pull.
RUSSELL	I pull it by the neck but you can pull it anywhere you want.
JANE	Are you listening to this, Bill?

JANE exits.

RUSSELL	Where's Carolyn?
BILL	In the basement.

RUSSELL sits. BILL drinks. RUSSELL watches.

RUSSELL	Pour me one?
BILL	Aren't you on medication?
RUSSELL	The Frenchman makes me drink milk.
BILL	Good. I approve.
RUSSELL	It's playin' havoc with my cholesterol.
BILL	I worry about you carrying wood.
RUSSELL	It's not as heavy as it looks.
BILL	You were seriously out of breath. What if you had a heart attack?
RUSSELL	I pop one of those little black pills the doctor gives me.
BILL	The nitroglycerine?
RUSSELL	That's the one. When I can't catch my breath, I just sit down and take one of those little black pills before I pass out.
BILL	How many do you take?
RUSSELL	Just one a day.
BILL	Dad. Those pills are for heart attacks!
RUSSELL	That's right. I have a heart attack every day. I'm running out. Can you write me a prescription?
BILL	No. You have to slow down.
RUSSELL	Slow down. Yeah. You said that before.
BILL	It's the truth.
RUSSELL	You learn the truth being a doctor?
BILL	I know what's good for you.
RUSSELL	All you know is how to keep me alive.
BILL	Isn't that the idea?
RUSSELL	But what am I being kept alive for? Eh? Besides the turkey dinner and the rhubarb pie. When the Eskimos got too old to work, they'd just crawl out of their igloos and walk off into the storm.

BILL	Into the storm?
RUSSELL	Yeah. "Into the storm." Well, maybe the storm isn't important. The point is, they made a decision and left.
BILL	Left and went where?
RUSSELL	The Hereafter. The Pearly Gates. The Hallelujah Chorus.
BILL	You're talking about dying.
RUSSELL	My God I'm glad you got a university education.
BILL	Dad. This "into the storm" business. You're not thinking of this for yourself, are you?
RUSSELL	No. I thought the cows might be interested. Of course me. I'm a burden, that's all, and when Carolyn has her baby it'll be worse. I was thinking I might go tonight. Wha'd'ya say?
BILL	Ohmigod.

BILL takes a large drink.

RUSSELL	Think it over.

RUSSELL gently takes BILL's glass...

It's a big decision.

...and drains it.

But I think those Eskimo lads were smart. When they couldn't hold a spear or pull a load, they'd just go out and wait for a polar bear to pick them up like a garbage truck.

BILL takes the glass but it's empty.

Why don't you get a refill.

BILL	Dad. They don't live like that anymore.
RUSSELL	They don't?
BILL	No. They're educated, modern people.
RUSSELL	With haemorrhoids?
BILL	Their old people don't walk off into storms to die.

RUSSELL	Lots of things change but they don't always get better. You have to wait a few years to realize that. Me, I'm off like old peaches. But don't tell the kids, okay? They wouldn't understand.
BILL	Look. I'll write you that prescription.
RUSSELL	You do that. Last thing I want to do is die of a heart attack.

The basement door opens. CAROLYN and MICHEL enter.

CAROLYN	Hi. We found the cranberry sauce. Where's Mum?
RUSSELL	She's in the powder room, pulling the duck.
CAROLYN	When she gets back, we'll eat.
BILL	Shouldn't you be sitting down?
CAROLYN	Gosh no. I'm fine. I hardly even notice that I'm pregnant. Wow. Does anyone else find it hot in here?

JANE enters.

RUSSELL	*(to MICHEL)* Bill needs another drink.
JANE	There you are darling. Are you all right? You look flushed. Why don't you sit down and let me handle it.
CAROLYN	Mum. You're the guest. I want you to sit down over there and relax.
JANE	But there's nothing going on over there. Besides, I feel badly watching you work. You must be so uncomfortable.
CAROLYN	Stop fussing. I feel fine. Dad, would you do the honours and carve the bird?

MICHEL passes BILL an old carving knife.

BILL	Me? That should be Michael's job.
MICHEL	I'm no good at carving.
CAROLYN	We don't eat meat very often.
BILL	It's not my place to carve.

CAROLYN	I'd like you to do it, Dad. I always remember you carving the Christmas turkey.
JANE	And you kids always used to fight over the drumstick.
CAROLYN	It was the only thing we were allowed to eat with our hands.
JANE	Your father used to carve the bird so thin and even.
CAROLYN	And that's why I wanted him to carve this evening.
JANE	Aw…
BILL	Is this the only knife you have?
CAROLYN	Is it not sharp enough?
BILL	The knife's fine but… Dad, do you remember the beautiful stag horn set you and Mum got as a wedding present.
RUSSELL	I still have it. *(everyone is pleased)*
CAROLYN	I've never seen it.
RUSSELL	That's 'cause I use it to split kindling. It's got a fine blade. If you hit a knot, it'll take a hammer.
BILL	So in other words, you've ruined it.
RUSSELL	I use it to split kindling, son, not stir paint.
BILL	Never mind.
RUSSELL	Oh no. If you want the knife, I'll get it for you.
BILL	This one is fine.
RUSSELL	It's no problem. I know exactly where it is.
	RUSSELL exits. Silence.
BILL	I'm sorry I brought it up.
CAROLYN	Don't worry. The arthritis makes him irritable.
BILL	I don't think it's the arthritis.
JANE	What's important is that we're all here, as a family. And soon there'll be one more. We should have a toast. Bill?
BILL	*(still thinking about his father)* What?

JANE	Didn't you bring some wine?
BILL	It's on the counter.
CAROLYN	Michel can open it.
BILL	It should be decanted.
JANE	Do we have to?
BILL	Go ahead. It's a '75 Lynch Bages but who cares.
CAROLYN	Sounds great.
BILL	Carolyn. Is Dad upset about something?
CAROLYN	He's upset about his hands and his heart and missing Nana and feeling useless but other than that he's fine.
BILL	Has he ever mentioned anything about the "Hereafter"?
CAROLYN	No.
MICHEL	Yes he does. He goes to the pantry and stands there yelling, "What am I here after?"
	Everyone laughs except BILL.
BILL	That's not what I mean. Dad just told me he's intending to walk out into a snowstorm and die.
	Silence.
JANE	Bill, I think you've had too much Scotch.
BILL	I have not.
CAROLYN	You can't always believe what he says, Dad.
JANE	I think you're a saint looking after your grandfather.
CAROLYN	It's a fair trade. *(gesturing proudly)* I get to live here.
JANE	Yes. Your father and I were just talking about that— wondering if there was some way we could help with the new house.
CAROLYN	We're fine, Mum.
BILL	See? She's fine.

JANE	But surely, there must be something we could pay for. A microwave, a cuisinart…
CAROLYN	No…
JANE	The roof.
CAROLYN	I've got everything I need. You're helping by being here, in my home… (*CAROLYN begins to have a contraction.*) Whoa…
MICHEL	Look at that. The baby's kicking.
BILL	Looks like the baby is playing a whole soccer game. When did you say you were due?
CAROLYN	Later. Mish.
MICHEL	I would like to propose a toast. To Bill and Jane, our guests and soon-to-be grandparents.
JANE	And to the baby.
ALL	To the baby.

> *They raise their glasses. CAROLYN gasps.*

JANE	What is it?
CAROLYN	I think something broke.
MICHEL	Really?
JANE	What broke?
MICHEL	Her wine glass.
CAROLYN	My wine glass?
MICHEL	(*emphatically*) Yes.
CAROLYN	(*not understanding but doing it anyway*) I broke my wine glass.
MICHEL	And now you have wine all over your dress.
CAROLYN	Which means I have to change! Oh well. Mish, could you help me? Mum, could you take the turkey out of the oven and start on the gravy. Don't worry. I'll be right back.

> *MICHEL and CAROLYN exit.*

BILL	That girl's in labour.
JANE	She's not in labour, she's just run off her feet.
BILL	How would you know?
JANE	Christmas Day, Labour Day, Every Day!

JANE begins cleaning up. RUSSELL enters.

RUSSELL	Here's the knife. *(BILL holds it up.)* I guess I did use it to stir paint.
BILL	I'll never get an edge on this.
RUSSELL	You will if you know how.
BILL	I know how.
RUSSELL	Then get to it.
BILL	I'll be here all night.
RUSSELL	If you don't want to do a little work.
BILL	I'm not afraid of work.
RUSSELL	Yeah. You acquired the knack for it on the bus to University.

BILL begins furiously to strop the knife on the steel. JANE has taken the turkey out of the oven.

JANE	There's not much fat from this bird.
BILL	It's not working.
RUSSELL	You're not doing it properly.
BILL	Then why don't you show me?
RUSSELL	*(holds up hands)* I can't.

BILL continues stropping. There is a knock on the door.

JANE	Bill, will you get the door? Russell?

They ignore her. She crosses and opens the door to DAWN Shaw, the midwife. She is middle-aged, dressed professionally but comfortably, is pulling

*a large, rolling suitcase and is obviously at home
in the house.*

DAWN	Hello.
JANE	Hello.
DAWN	I'm Dawn Shaw.
JANE	Yes.
DAWN	You must be Mrs. Bingham.
JANE	Yes. Are you here for dinner?
DAWN	No, I'm here to see Carolyn.
JANE	Carolyn's busy right now. Are you a friend?
DAWN	No, I'm Carolyn's—
RUSSELL	*(interrupting)* Sweetie!
JANE	Excuse me.
RUSSELL	You made it.
DAWN	Weren't you expecting me?
RUSSELL	I sure was. You bet.
JANE	Bill? *(still sharpening)* Bill!
BILL	What?
JANE	We have a guest.
BILL	Very glad to meet you. Would you like a glass of wine? Please, sit down. *(to RUSSELL)* See? It's dull as dishwater.
RUSSELL	Son. Forget the knife. This is Dawn. She's my girlfriend.
DAWN	Mr. Bingham!
RUSSELL	Call me Russell.
JANE	So you do have a hobby.
DAWN	I think Russell is pulling your leg, Mrs. Bingham. I deliver babies.

RUSSELL	Oh no.
JANE	Then you must be Carolyn's doctor.
BILL	Is there something wrong?
DAWN	No, there's nothing wrong. At least I don't think so. But I'm not really a doctor.
BILL	You're not?
DAWN	No, I'm a—
RUSSELL	*(loudly)* Vet!
JANE & BILL	A vet?
RUSSELL	Yeah. She's not my girlfriend. She's the vet.
BILL	She said she delivers babies.
RUSSELL	That's right. She's here to deliver a baby cow.
BILL	In the middle of winter?
RUSSELL	Oh yeah. We calve twelve months a year nowadays. Steroids. But we don't want the cow to calve, see, because you're here, see, so we called Dawn out and after dinner she's going to stop it.
BILL	Stop the cow's labour.
RUSSELL	Yup.
BILL	*(to DAWN)* How do you stop a cow's labour?
DAWN	*(at a loss)* Breath control...?
BILL	Really.
RUSSELL	Oh there's been some big changes since you been in the barn, Billy, big changes.
BILL	I'm glad you're a vet. For a second I thought you were a midwife. It's just the kind of nutty thing my daughter would do. Hire a midwife.
DAWN	You don't approve of midwives?
BILL	They're fine as long as you don't mind gambling with a baby's life.

RUSSELL	A midwife birthed me in that room right over there. It wasn't gambling then. And now Carolyn is going to have her baby in— *(He stops himself.)*
BILL	A hospital.
RUSSELL	Yeah.
BILL	A modern, well-equipped, professionally staffed hospital. *(to DAWN)* It's an easy choice to make, isn't it?
DAWN	I know what I'd choose.
BILL	Exactly. But you wouldn't believe the risks people are willing to take just for a little novelty.
RUSSELL	When I was born everyone had their babies at home. All the neighbourhood women brought food and the men would help with chores. Everyone came together. Of course, you'd lose one or two along the way, but then you'd just make another one. As I remember, making them was the best part.
BILL	No one's willing to lose one anymore, Dad. Believe me. Parents want perfection. Every single time.

CAROLYN and MICHEL enter.

JANE	Here she is. Oh honey, you look so pale.
CAROLYN	I'm fine.
JANE	Your friend is here.
RUSSELL	Your friend the vet.
CAROLYN	Hi Dawn.
DAWN	Hi Carolyn.
MICHEL	Hi Dawn.
DAWN	Hi Michel.
BILL	She's going to use breath control on a cow. I'm going to watch.
CAROLYN	Let me get dinner on the table.

JANE	Nonsense. Michel and I can manage the dinner. You sit there next to your friend.
DAWN	Yes. Sit next to me.
JANE	Michel, can you set a place setting for Dawn?
MICHEL	Sure.
JANE	Bill, can you take the bird to the table.

CAROLYN crosses to the sofa, BILL to the kitchen.

DAWN	How fast are the contractions coming?
CAROLYN	Every eight minutes.
DAWN	Can I do an internal?
CAROLYN	Now?!
DAWN	Carolyn, you're in labour.
CAROLYN	No, I'm not.
DAWN	Ask your parents to leave.
CAROLYN	They just got here.
DAWN	Yes, they're here but now I'm here, and I can't pretend I'm a vet.
JANE	Dinner is served.

Scene Three – The Dinner

*Music. A few bars of Handel's "Hallelujah Chorus".
CAROLYN moves to the table.*

JANE	Do you have a seating plan?
CAROLYN	Yes. I want Michel and me at the ends with Mum and Dad on his left and right. Dawn and Grampa, you're next to me.

They arrange themselves and sit.

JANE	Don't you think your father should be at the head of the table. You did ask him to carve.
CAROLYN	Okay.
JANE	And shouldn't I be at this end so I can serve?
CAROLYN	Okay.
JANE	Then you can sit next to your father with Dawn and your grandfather and Michel can sit next to me.

They arrange themselves and sit.

CAROLYN	This is just like at home.
JANE	Yes. It makes more sense, don't you think?
CAROLYN	No. I want Michel at the head of the table.
JANE	But that's your father's...
CAROLYN	I want you to sit over there.
JANE	But—
CAROLYN	Please.
JANE	All right.
CAROLYN	Dad, you can sit on the side, but carve at the end.
BILL	But...
JANE	Whatever she says.
CAROLYN	Grampa, sit over there please.

They move and sit.

Thank you. Okay. Mish?

MICHEL	Ready.
CAROLYN	Go.

MICHEL begins to serve. As each bowl and plate is served there are ooohs and aaahs of appreciation.

Here are the vegetables—roast carrots, potatoes, leeks and, for Dad, rutabagas. They're all from my garden.

JANE	What an interesting way to cut carrots.

l to r: Caroline Gillis, Ross Manson, Shawn Mathieson,
Mary Krohnert, Jerry Franken, Michelle Fisk

Photograph by Terry Manzo, Stratford

CAROLYN	Grampa did them.
RUSSELL	Special knife.
CAROLYN	Here's dill pickles, cranberry sauce and wild grape jelly all homemade. Mum, I used your savory and apple stuffing recipe for the turkey. Apples from the old Mac tree.
BILL	Is that tree still alive?
RUSSELL	It is now.
CAROLYN	The roots were good so I trimmed it back and now it's bearing.
BILL	I remember Mum making baked apples from that tree.
RUSSELL	I guess old trees have got some use.
BILL	Yeah, if they're trimmed back.

CAROLYN	Tell everyone about the turkey, Grampa.
RUSSELL	Corn fed.
JANE	I thought you were vegetarian.
CAROLYN	I am. His name was Tom. I won't be having any.
RUSSELL	He was a good lad, Tom was. And died like a trooper.

MICHEL produces a dried flower centrepiece.

CAROLYN	Here's the centrepiece. These are all dried flowers from the flower garden.
JANE	Even the silver dollars?
CAROLYN	Yes. I had them under glass right 'til the end of June and then... then...

She begins to have a small contraction.

MICHEL	The pie.
CAROLYN	Right. And for dessert we have rhubarb pie.
RUSSELL	Lorna Bingham's Red Ribbon.
MICHEL	Best pie ever made. From the famous Bingham rhubarb, frozen last spring, and served tonight with our own raw milk cheese on the side. Voila.
CAROLYN	Enjoy.
JANE	Darling. Everything you've done. It's perfect.
CAROLYN	It was no trouble at all. Grampa. Will you say grace?
RUSSELL	I will. *(He stands and clears his throat.)*
MICHEL	Make it short.
RUSSELL	You'll want it in Latin?
CAROLYN	*(warning)* Grampa.
RUSSELL	Let us pray. Dear Lord, we thank You for the bounty of this table and the many other meals over many years we have enjoyed by Your grace. We remember those present, those departed and the one who will soon be among us. I thank You for the blessing of my grand-daughter and pray that she'll serve Christian food

more often and none of that *toy-few*. Bless Lord our prosperity and open our hearts to those who may be hungry or cold on this winter night. We ask this humbly in Your name. Amen.

ALL   Amen.

Everyone sighs into the fullness of the moment.

RUSSELL   And please Lord perform a miracle on the carving knife because the way my son sharpened it, it won't cut the cock off a jellyfish.

Shrieks of laughter and mock outrage. BILL attacks the bird. Everyone passes bowls.

MICHEL   Let's eat.

JANE   Russell, how could you ruin such a beautiful grace.

RUSSELL   He'd have better luck with a chainsaw.

CAROLYN   You watch. Dad is the best carver in the world. What's the matter Dad?

BILL   I'm afraid the bird's not done.

CAROLYN   What?!

JANE   The oven was hot when I checked.

BILL   I'm sorry but there's not enough cooked to make a meal.

CAROLYN   I put it in at the right time. Grampa said twenty minutes to the pound.

JANE   That's right.

CAROLYN   Twenty minutes times eight pounds.

BILL   This turkey weighs a lot more than eight pounds. It's more like eight kilograms.

JANE   Is that what you did, darling? Confuse pounds with kilograms?

CAROLYN   Grampa?

RUSSELL   Don't ask me about kilograms.

BILL   A kilogram is 2.2 pounds. You might have learned that
              if you'd stayed in University.

              CAROLYN stands.

JANE   Carolyn, it doesn't matter.

CAROLYN   Yes it does. It matters a great deal.

              She exits to RUSSELL's bedroom.

DAWN   Excuse me.

              *She follows CAROLYN with her midwife bag. The
              door closes.*

JANE   Bill. Sometimes I could just wring your neck.

BILL   Because she can't cook a turkey?

JANE   Have you seen nothing that's gone on here tonight?
              The work, the care, the love that went into this meal.
              And her nine months pregnant.

BILL   I should have stayed in the car.

RUSSELL   It's warmer in the barn. With the turkeys.

BILL   You just can't leave well enough alone, can you?

JANE   Look who's talking.

              *BILL takes a wine glass and moves downstage.
              MICHEL goes to the bedroom door and knocks.*

MICHEL   Caro?

              *The door opens and he exits into the bedroom. We see
              him embrace CAROLYN.*

RUSSELL   Janey—could I have some potatoes, please?

              She serves him.

              You have to mash them.

              She mashes.

              With butter.

              She adds butter and mashes.

              Could you move that rhubarb pie into the oven?

JANE   Yes.

RUSSELL   I've got something to tell you.

JANE   Not now.

RUSSELL   Because you're good with tradition.

JANE   Please Russell.

RUSSELL   It's important.

JANE   Eat your potatoes.

RUSSELL   It might be my last chance. *(He coughs.)*

JANE   What is it?

RUSSELL   When the Binghams came over from Scotland, the
            only thing they brought with them was rhubarb and
            dysentery. The ones who survived the dysentery
            planted the rhubarb right outside that window next to
            the well. It's been growing there ever since.

JANE   I know. You'd think the Binghams invented rhubarb.

RUSSELL   Around here we like to think we did. 'Cause my Lorna
            made the best rhubarb pie in the county. Red Ribbon
            every year. But when she passed on, there was no
            recipe. Carolyn and I've baked over a hundred rhubarb
            pies trying to find her secret and Janey, that pie, that
            pie in the oven right over there, is the perfect match.

JANE   That's a lovely story.

RUSSELL   The story's not important. Stories get forgotten. But the
            recipe.... Look. Carolyn wrote it out fine and *(passing
            an envelope)* I want you to keep it. It's the way I want
            Lorna and me to be remembered.

JANE   You want to be remembered for a pie?

RUSSELL   Better than a tombstone. In fact you can skip the
            tombstone. Rhubarb pie is sweet and sour. Just like
            life. Bake it in remembrance of us. So long.

JANE   Where are you going?

RUSSELL   Bill knows.

JANE	Bill, Russell says he's leaving.
BILL	No, he's not.
RUSSELL	Yes I am. I'm leaving you with the bill for the new septic tank.
JANE	We want to pay for the roof.
RUSSELL	The roof is cheap. Pay for the well and the septic tank. Then you've got it coming and going.
BILL	I'm not paying for anything.
RUSSELL	You will.

The wind blows.

Stormy night. Good night to make a crossing. Wind like that, blow your soul straight to heaven.

In the bedroom.

CAROLYN	Here it comes. Big one. *(gently)* Ow, ow, ow, ow, ow.
DAWN	Breathe, breathe, breathe…
MICHEL	Okay, okay, okay…

The contraction passes.

DAWN	How was that?
CAROLYN	Fabulous.
DAWN	Really?
CAROLYN	When it stops, it's fabulous.
DAWN	You're doing great.
CAROLYN	How long have I got?
DAWN	You're four centimetres dilated. When you reach ten you can start pushing.
CAROLYN	So how long 'till then?
DAWN	As long as it takes. I'd say you're moving along beautifully.
CAROLYN	Yes but do I have an hour? Half an hour? Can I at least serve the pie?

DAWN	Carolyn. This is it. You're in labour.
CAROLYN	It's over, isn't it?
DAWN	The pretending? Yes. The pretending is over.
CAROLYN	Why is it that when you really, really want something to go right, the wanting somehow makes it go wrong?
DAWN	You need to think about your baby.
CAROLYN	Damn turkey.
DAWN	The baby.
CAROLYN	What am I going to tell my parents?
MICHEL	Caro, this was going to be our time. Us and the baby. I don't want them here if they're not on our side.
CAROLYN	So they have to leave?
MICHEL	Yes.
CAROLYN	'Cause there's no other choice.
MICHEL	No.
CAROLYN	Because I'm in labour.
MICHEL	Right.

Silence.

CAROLYN	I can't do it.
MICHEL	Then let me tell them.
CAROLYN	Really?
MICHEL	Why not?
CAROLYN	They'll hate you.
DAWN	Why don't I tell them. It might be easier coming from me.
CAROLYN	What would you say?
DAWN	I would explain that you've chosen a home birth and you would like them to leave.
CAROLYN	But that's the truth.

DAWN	Yes.
CAROLYN	I can't tell them the truth.
DAWN	Why not?
CAROLYN	It's rude. Tell them I'm sick.
DAWN	But you're not.
CAROLYN	I know, but the truth is so... truthful. You have to shroud it, whitewash it, put lipstick on it.
MICHEL	Why?
CAROLYN	Because they can't handle it.
MICHEL	Caro! You don't need to look after them. You need to look after yourself.
CAROLYN	I know.
MICHEL	You're in charge. You're the boss. If you want, you can go out there and tell them, tell them to *pees off*.
CAROLYN	I can't tell them that.
MICHEL	But you could if you want.
CAROLYN	Because I'm da boss.
MICHEL	Voila.
CAROLYN	Okay. I'll tell them.
DAWN	Good for you.
CAROLYN	*(She gasps.)* Oh no.
MICHEL	What?
CAROLYN	I have to call your mother.
MICHEL	My mother?
CAROLYN	I promised I'd tell her when the labour started.
MICHEL	Let's pretend you forgot.
CAROLYN	That's a lie. And I'm not lying anymore.
DAWN	Atta' girl.

l to r: Caroline Gillis, Mary Krohnert, Shawn Mathieson

MICHEL	You want me to tell my mother in Quebec before you tell your parents in the next room.
CAROLYN	I'm da boss.
MICHEL	Okay. I'll tell my mother.

> *MICHEL returns to the kitchen. JANE and BILL stand expectantly.*

	Hi. I just have to make a phone call.

> *MICHEL picks up the phone and dials. We hear a contraction from the other room.*

BILL	Michael. What's going on?
MICHEL	Going on? Nothing. Carolyn's just…
JANE	Just…?
BILL	Just…?

MICHEL	Upset about the turkey. She wants me to call my mother to…
JANE	To…?
BILL	To…?
MICHEL	Get her recipe for tourtière. (*on the telephone*) *Allo mama? C'est commencé.* // *La chose.* // *La chose qu'on attendait.* // *Oui.* // Okay. // Okay. // Okay. // *Salut.*

> *He hangs up. BILL and JANE are still watching.*

BILL & JANE	Well?
MICHEL	That was my mother. She says hello.

> *The door opens. CAROLYN enters supported by DAWN.*

CAROLYN	Hi Dad. Mum.
BILL	Carolyn, what's going on?
CAROLYN	It looks like I got the timing wrong on more than the turkey. I'm in labour.
BILL	I knew it.
JANE	That's wonderful.
BILL	Don't you worry. I'll warm up the car. And I'll call the hospital so they're ready.
CAROLYN	I'm not going to the hospital.
BILL	I don't see any reason to wait. You can get checked in, get settled…
CAROLYN	What I mean is, I'm going to have the baby here.
BILL	Here? How are you going to do that?
CAROLYN	I need to sit down.
DAWN	Dr. Bingham, Mrs. Bingham, I'm Carolyn and Michel's midwife. I've been retained because they want to have their baby here, in their home.
JANE	Oh, Carolyn.

CAROLYN	I'm sorry, Dad. I didn't want you to know.
BILL	I can understand why.
CAROLYN	I didn't want to hurt you.
BILL	Never mind me, Carolyn. What about the baby?
DAWN	Carolyn is completely healthy, Doctor. The baby is presenting normally. Every indication is for a normal birth.
BILL	There is nothing normal about having a baby in a bedroom.
DAWN	Is it more normal on an operating table?
BILL	It's safer and that's all that matters.
DAWN	You think a hospital is safe?
MICHEL	Please. This is our choice.
CAROLYN	And everything's going to be fine.
BILL	You don't know that. No one knows that.
DAWN	Doctor, I can see you're upset.
BILL	Don't patronize me. We will have no tragedies here.
CAROLYN	Mummy…
JANE	Your father's a doctor.
DAWN	Carolyn, let me reassure you. The baby is not at risk.
BILL	Don't listen to her. These men track in manure from a barn. God knows what germs are in here.
DAWN	Carolyn is used to the germs here and *not* used to the germs in a hospital.
BILL	That's rubbish.
RUSSELL	I was born in this house. And you were brought up in this house. And I don't remember any germs getting us.
BILL	None of you know what you're talking about.
JANE	Bill, you're yelling.

BILL	Of course I'm yelling. *(pleading)* Why didn't you come to me, Carolyn? Why didn't you ask my advice instead of going to a stranger?
CAROLYN	Dawn is more family to me than you are, Daddy. She's kinder and more supportive and she respects my opinions.
BILL	Even if they're wrong.
JANE	Bill, we should go.
BILL	Why should we leave?
DAWN	We need to have quiet.
RUSSELL	You've come to the wrong place for quiet.
BILL	If there's anyone who should be leaving it's her.
JANE	Bill, please.
RUSSELL	Now listen here, sonny Jim.
DAWN	I've been retained by Carolyn and Michel.
BILL	Are you trying to be a lawyer?
RUSSELL	I was born in this house. Born in that room.
BILL	Dad, will you stay out of this?
JANE	Couldn't we just sit down and talk?

The following is spoken all together.

BILL	Jane. All of you. Will you listen? *(DAWN starts.)* Listen. Please listen. I am a doctor. This situation is unsafe. We must move to a hospital. *(RUSSELL starts.)* That is the only reasonable course of action. Listen. *(JANE starts.)* This patient is not in her right mind. She needs medical help. We have to leave. Right away. Right now. Because having a baby in this house is dangerous, irresponsible…
DAWN	I have been retained, in writing, and Doctor you have no right to interfere. Your relationship with this patient totally compromises your ability to clinically analyze the risk. You are completely overreacting and I must ask you to leave for the good of the mother and child.

Do you hear me, Doctor. You must leave and leave now.

RUSSELL   Hey now listen, this is still my house, you know, and I don't have to listen to you ordering me around. I remember you as a baby. Yes I do. Mewling and puking. You used to eat worms. No I won't be quiet. There's nothing wrong with having a baby in this house. Nothing wrong at all.

JANE   Oh please, everyone stop arguing, I hate arguing, and you're upsetting Carolyn. Please Bill, you're upsetting her. Russell, please be quiet. Dawn, we must sit down. I'm going to cry. What am I saying? Everyone sit down! Everyone be quiet! Bill, Russell, hush.

Climaxing with...

DAWN   Leave, leave, leave, leave, leave.

BILL   Listen, listen, listen, listen, listen.

RUSSELL   Nothing, nothing, nothing.

JANE   Quiet, quiet, quiet, quiet.

MICHEL   *(standing on a chair) Taissez-vous!!!*

Silence.

CAROLYN   The baby can hear this, you know. The baby can hear your loud, angry voices. I wanted everything about this birth to be filled with love and kindness, but instead we have yelling and tension and now my labour has stopped.... The baby must be so frightened. And I don't blame him. Listening to you, I wouldn't want to be born.

Musical sting.

End of Act I

ACT II

Scene One – The Discussion

> *A few minutes later. RUSSELL, BILL and JANE are standing as they were at the end of Act I. DAWN is kneeling in front of CAROLYN listening to the baby's heartbeat with a stethoscope. MICHEL is holding CAROLYN's hand.*

DAWN   The baby's fine.

CAROLYN   Are you sure?

DAWN   Steady, slow heartbeat.

CAROLYN   Not frightened?

DAWN   I'd say baby's having a nap.

> *BILL clears his throat. Everyone watches.*

BILL   Carolyn.

CAROLYN   *(ready for anything)* Yes Father?

> *BILL hesitates, looks at JANE. JANE glares.*

BILL   Nothing.

CAROLYN   I'm going to lie down.

> *CAROLYN exits to the downstairs bedroom and shuts the door.*

> *MICHEL exits to the bedroom and shuts the door.*

> *DAWN goes to exit into the bedroom but changes her mind. Instead, she gets a chair and sits in front of the door.*

RUSSELL   Has anybody looked at the pie?

JANE   Russell.

BILL   Dad.

DAWN   Dr. Bingham, Mrs. Bingham, in the interest of Carolyn's baby, I think you should both leave.

BILL   Us? You're the one who should be leaving.

DAWN   But clearly you are in the middle of something to which you were not invited.

JANE   I was invited. We both were. Weren't we Bill?

DAWN   You were invited to dinner. The dinner is over.

BILL   Even if Carolyn were not my daughter, legally I am compelled to stay. If anything happened I would be liable.

DAWN   You think she's going to sue you?

BILL   She won't have to because she's going to the hospital.

DAWN   (lowering her voice) But the only problem here is you. You are totally stressing her out.

BILL   Is that a medical diagnosis?

DAWN   Please, let's not make this an ego thing. I just want what's best for the birth and the best thing is for you guys to leave.

JANE   Is that what Carolyn wants?

BILL   You can't ask Carolyn.

JANE   Is it?

DAWN   (ignoring BILL) Carolyn, doesn't want to hurt your feelings. That's why she tried to hide her labour, but now, yes, she wants you to go.

JANE   I didn't hear her say that.

DAWN   It's so obvious.

JANE   Not to me and I'm her mother. How do you know what she wants?

BILL   She's in labour. She doesn't know what she wants.

JANE   Bill.

DAWN   How did you ever become a doctor?

BILL	Because I was damn smart and worked damn hard.
RUSSELL	Hah!
BILL	What?
RUSSELL	Nothing.
BILL	Let's get this straight. Carolyn's going to the hospital.
DAWN	But why?
BILL	One. Because her waters have broken. That means infection could start any minute. Two. Her labour has stopped. Was that brought on by a family argument or foetal distress? Prudence dictates we move the patient to a hospital and get her labour started.
DAWN	With drugs.
BILL	With medication. What do you recommend? A drive down a bumpy road?
DAWN	Carolyn doesn't need intervention.
BILL	You'd just leave her?
DAWN	There's no need to rush. Carolyn can deliver her own baby in her own time. All she needs is the support of the people in this room.
BILL	And the baby? What sort of "support" do you have for the child.
DAWN	Name it.
BILL	The baby's not breathing.
DAWN	I carry oxygen.
BILL	The mother haemorrhages.
DAWN	I carry pitocin.
BILL	The cord is wrapped around the baby's neck.
DAWN	I'll unwrap it.
BILL	Breech birth.
DAWN	It's not.

BILL	You have a portable ultra sound? How can you be sure of the presentation?
DAWN	*(holding out her hands)* With these, Doctor. Remember using these? They can tell you a lot. Carolyn is presenting normally. I guarantee it.
BILL	Then you're pretty damn good. Because where I work, surrounded by a billion dollar health facility, I can't guarantee a thing.

Stand off.

DAWN	All right. I can't guarantee anything—but I've helped hundreds of women give birth, some of them in mud huts filled with smoke and flies and animals and all I had was knowledge and these hands. But the women... the women were strong in their homes, surrounded by their family...
BILL	And none of them required surgery?
DAWN	Far fewer than here. I've seen women perform miracles.
BILL	What about the ones who didn't perform miracles?
DAWN	Some babies died.
BILL	Right, and that's not going to happen to my grandchild.

BILL goes to the telephone.

JANE	Bill, what are you doing?
BILL	Calling an ambulance.
JANE	*(worried)* Bill...
BILL	I'm going to have the paramedics throw this woman into the snow. Hello, this is Dr. William Bingham. I have a mother with foetal distress. I'll need an ambulance—

JANE strides over and disconnects the phone.

(astonished) What are you doing?

JANE	If you force Carolyn to go to a hospital against her will, we will lose her, lose her forever.

BILL	Is everyone here mad?
RUSSELL	I'd say so.
BILL	Dad, will you shut up?
JANE	Don't raise your voice.
BILL	Raise my voice? I'm going to raise the bloody roof.
JANE	She can hear you.
BILL	I want her to hear me. I want her to come out here and do what she's told. But she won't because she's never done what she's told.
RUSSELL	And where did she get that from?
BILL & RUSSELL	*(pointing at each other)* You!
BILL	All right. That's it.

> BILL goes after RUSSELL.

JANE	Bill, stop.

> The following three speeches spoken together.

RUSSELL	*(fleeing)* Because you never did what you were told. Not once! Not once, not once…
BILL	It's about time you had some respect for what I am and what I say…
JANE	Stop it. Both of you. Stop it right this minute. Stoooooooooop…

> CAROLYN tears the door open. RUSSELL, BILL and JANE freeze. BILL is standing on a chair.

CAROLYN	Grampa, are you okay?
RUSSELL	Oh, just fine.
CAROLYN	Mum?
JANE	We were just having a little discussion.
CAROLYN	*(disgusted)* You're all lying.

> CAROLYN exits. RUSSELL sits, panting.

Photograph by Terry Manzo, Stratford

l to r: Jerry Franken, Michelle Fisk, Ross Manson, Mary Krohnert, Caroline Gillis

BILL	Are you all right?
RUSSELL	Take more than a kid to scare me.
BILL	I feel like I'm sixteen all over again.
JANE	I think we should go but I want to stay.
RUSSELL	I was born in that room. My mother wanted my dad to fetch the midwife, but the mare went lame. Whenever my dad had to pay for something, the mare went lame. So my mother told my sister and she ran the whole way.
	My dad built this house but my mother filled it. And Lorna filled it. But most of all, Carolyn fills it.

Scene Two – A Biscuit Case

Bedroom.

CAROLYN   (*listening at the door*) Thank God, they've stopped.
I remember when I was a little girl, they used to argue
like that. I used to hide in my closet, with my hands
over my ears and my knees over my hands trying not
to hear. But I heard. Daddy's angry roaring and
Mummy's nag, nag, nag. And finally, when I couldn't
take it any longer, when I thought my whole life was
going to rip apart, I would throw open their door and
storm into their room screaming, "Stop fighting, stop
fighting, stop fighting" and they'd stand, frozen until
my mother said, very calmly, "we're not fighting dear,
we're just having a little discussion."

MICHEL   They're crazy.

CAROLYN   But don't you see. If they're crazy, I must be crazy too.

MICHEL   You're not crazy.

CAROLYN   I am. Everything I've done in my life—moving out
here, living with Grampa, making rhubarb chutney—
everything has been trying to prove that I am not
them. Isn't that being crazy?

MICHEL   Sit down.

CAROLYN   If I sit down, I'll never get up.

MICHEL   You don't need to get up.

CAROLYN   I want the baby to come.

MICHEL   He will.

    She sits.

CAROLYN   I feel like a beached whale.

MICHEL   Relax.

CAROLYN   I'm as big as a barn and fat as a cow.

MICHEL   I love you.

CAROLYN	You don't. You can't. I must look so ugly.
MICHEL	You are the mother of my child, my life partner and my love.
CAROLYN	Really? (MICHEL nods.) Okay, that's good. What you just said? That was really good. Oh Mish. You are so not like my father. (suddenly) Oh! My! Gosh!
MICHEL	What?
CAROLYN	What if the only reason I love you is because you're not like my father.
MICHEL	Caro…
CAROLYN	But don't you see? It makes perfect sense. You're French. He's English. You love the farm. He hates the farm. You make me feel good and he drives me crazy.
MICHEL	You're not crazy.
CAROLYN	Are you sure?
MICHEL	Well, sometimes, you are a bit of a biscuit case.
CAROLYN	Basket case.
MICHEL	What?
CAROLYN	Not a biscuit case. A basket case.
MICHEL	What's crazy about a basket?
CAROLYN	I don't know.
MICHEL	Look. I love you. Do you love me?
CAROLYN	Yes.
MICHEL	So. You have a baby. I milk some cows. We have a life. Why do you make things so crazy?
CAROLYN	I make them crazy because I am—
MICHEL	(interrupting) Uh!
CAROLYN	A biscuit case.
MICHEL	It makes sense, no? A basket is useful but a biscuit is flaky.

CAROLYN	So I'm a flake.
MICHEL	Sometimes.
CAROLYN	Is that why you didn't marry me?
MICHEL	Me? I was the one who proposed.
CAROLYN	Only once.
MICHEL	On my knees.
CAROLYN	I just couldn't bear dealing with Mother. The biggest day in her life was getting married and the next biggest day is getting me married. In her wedding dress.
MICHEL	So. After the baby we'll tie the rope.
CAROLYN	Tie the knot.
MICHEL	Knot?! How can you tie a knot into a knot? You have to tie a rope into a knot.
CAROLYN	Let's do it now.
MICHEL	What?
CAROLYN	Get married.
MICHEL	Now?
CAROLYN	Yeah.
MICHEL	Here?
CAROLYN	Yeah.

MICHEL laughs.

I'm serious. It's a symbol. A symbol that we are a family. First us, then with the baby.

MICHEL	Caro, when women have babies sometimes their minds—
CAROLYN	If you think I want to get married because of hormones I'm gonna pull your bottom lip over your head and give you a taste of childbirth. I want to get married.
MICHEL	Okay.
CAROLYN	Right now.

MICHEL	No problem
CAROLYN	In a wedding dress.
MICHEL	Why not?
CAROLYN	That would make me so happy.
MICHEL	Okay, one wedding coming up.

Scene Three – The Kitchen

*Light up stage right. MICHEL enters the kitchen.
Everyone stands expectantly.*

MICHEL	Hi.
JANE	How's Carolyn?
MICHEL	Good. Good. Really good.
BILL	Has the labour started?
MICHEL	Labour? Oh yes. No. No labour.
DAWN	How is she feeling?
MICHEL	*(carefully)* She's feeling… a lot of things.

Everyone nods.

Excuse me.

He crosses to RUSSELL.

(sotto voce) Russell.

RUSSELL	Yeah?
MICHEL	I need a wedding dress.
RUSSELL	Oh yeah.
MICHEL	Right now.
RUSSELL	What for?

*BILL and JANE lean in. MICHEL looks at them.
They lean back.*

MICHEL	For a wedding.
RUSSELL	Oh. I've got Lorna's wedding dress.
MICHEL	You do?
RUSSELL	Well, it's not something I'd ever use for rags.
MICHEL	Can I borrow it?
RUSSELL	It won't fit you.
MICHEL	It's for Carolyn.
RUSSELL	It won't fit her either. Lorna wasn't pregnant when she got married. We did things in the right order.
JANE	Is someone getting married?
MICHEL	No. *(to RUSSELL)* Where's the dress?

RUSSELL opens the blanket box/trunk that has been acting as the coffee table centre stage. RUSSELL pulls out a dress box and hands it to MICHEL.

I need a Bible.

JANE	What for?
MICHEL	Well, the baby is not coming so we wanted to make a prayer to God for help and having a Bible would make it a good prayer, like an amplified prayer so it would go straight to God, you know? Direct, ping, right into God's head and then... well then he has to help and we have a baby. Where's the Bible?
RUSSELL	In my room, by my bed, where I never read it.

MICHEL exits to the house.

JANE	Something's going on.
BILL	Rank superstition, that's what.
JANE	Russell, what was in that box?
RUSSELL	I'm not saying.
JANE	They're getting married, aren't they?
DAWN	If they are, it's a private ceremony.

JANE	(to BILL) She can't get married in a bedroom. Even Russell didn't get married in a bedroom.
RUSSELL	That's right. We had a church wedding.
JANE	That's what I want for Carolyn. With bridesmaids and flowers and a three-tier wedding cake and my daughter wearing *my* wedding dress.
BILL	They're not having a real wedding.
DAWN	It could be real. It could be very real.
JANE	What do you know about weddings? You probably got married under an oak tree wearing a cheap Indian print dress with hippies in blue jeans and sandals playing "Give Peace a Chance" on out-of-tune guitars. You probably made up your own vows.
DAWN	That's pretty close.
JANE	I know your type. You don't do anything properly.
	MICHEL re-enters, grabs the telephone, and then tries to exit.
	(sweetly) Michel?
MICHEL	Yes.
JANE	Is there anything that Carolyn would like her mother to do?
MICHEL	Uh. No.
	He exits immediately trailing the wire from the telephone receiver.
JANE	Bill. Go in there and stop them.
BILL	I'll stop the home birth. You stop the home wedding.
RUSSELL	Relax Janey. Who cares how they do it, as long as they do it. Life is simple. Birth, marriage, death. In between there's work and, with luck, some good eating. So why don't we celebrate? Why don't we have a nice piece of rhubarb pie.
JANE	I'm going to take your rhubarb pie and shove it down your damn, damn, damn, damn, damn, damn throat.

Everyone is stunned.

(*pleading*) I want to be in there.

BILL	Jane, control yourself.
JANE	What's the matter Bill? Are you afraid I'm going to lose it? Are you afraid I'm going to fall apart? Are you afraid I'm going to freak out for the first time in thirty-three years?
DAWN	You tell him, sister.
JANE	(*fury*) Shut up! You're just what my daughter always wanted in a mother. A feminist. (*shocked*) Oh God. I'm making a scene. (*a little petulant*) Why shouldn't she wear my wedding dress? That was all I ever wanted. Remember, Bill? Belgian lace across the chest and bead work down the arms. It's still in style except for the hem line and she would look so beautiful.
BILL	(*gently*) Honey, the dress wouldn't fit. She's nine months pregnant.
JANE	(*ironic*) Bill, do you have any idea what this means to me?
BILL	(*low, intense*) Of course I do. But don't you see? Carolyn is doing it again. First to me, by having a home birth, and now to you by having a home wedding. She's doing exactly what it takes to drive us crazy.
JANE	(*rallying*) My God you're right.
BILL	(*firmly*) Don't let her get to you.
JANE	We're the parents.
BILL	She's the daughter.
JANE	(*slipping*) But why isn't she asking for me? Why isn't she coming out and saying, "Mum, I'm getting married and I need you to help me with the flowers, and the bridesmaids, and brushing my hair up in a French chignon." Why isn't she saying "I need you. I'll always need you."

> *She cries. The oven timer buzzes.*

RUSSELL   That'll be the pie.

Scene Four – The Wedding

> *CAROLYN and MICHEL are sitting side by side with a hand on the Bible between them. CAROLYN is wearing her grandmother's veil and the wedding dress is on her lap. As the lights come up, they are humming Wagner's "Bridal Chorus" (Here Comes the Bride).*

MICHEL   Will you Carolyn Lorna Bingham take me Michel Eustace Charbonneau to be your lawful wedded husband. To have and to hold, in sickness and in health, in love and in anger, in debt and in… we'll always be in debt.

CAROLYN   I know.

MICHEL   I'm sorry.

CAROLYN   I don't care.

MICHEL   You could have had more.

CAROLYN   I have more. More than enough.

MICHEL   Do you accept all this 'til death do us part?

CAROLYN   I do. Will you Mish love me Caro as I am, broken and whole, strong and weak, in the morning before coffee and at night when my feet are cold, when I feel like it and when I don't, and be faithful to me alone… unless I die first in which case I think you should re-marry because it would be good for you as long as it's not some cutesy-pie like that girl you were going out with before you met me because—

> *MICHEL stops her.*

Am I enough?

MICHEL	Yes. You and the baby and the cows are more than enough.
CAROLYN	Are there any persons present who have any objections to this marriage?
	They look around the empty room.
MICHEL	I now pronounce us man and wife.
CAROLYN	You may kiss the bride.
	MICHEL raises her veil and leans across her belly. They kiss. We hear MICHEL's mother's voice on the telephone.
MICHEL	*(on the telephone) Salut, Ma. On est marrié. Carolyn est assez belle. Elle apporte la robe de marriage de sa grand-mère et...//* Okay.
	He passes the phone to CAROLYN.
CAROLYN	Hello Maman. *(She kisses MICHEL.)* Merci. *(She kisses MICHEL.)* Au revoir.
	She passes the phone back.
MICHEL	*Faut que j'aille. //* Okay, okay, okay, *salut.*
	He hangs up.
CAROLYN	I love your family.
MICHEL	So do I. Me in Ontario. Them in Quebec.
CAROLYN	Hello husband.
MICHEL	Hello wife.
CAROLYN	What's wrong?
MICHEL	Nothing.
CAROLYN	Are you worried about the baby? *(MICHEL nods.)* Do you want to go to the hospital? *(He shrugs his shoulders.)* It's not what we imagined, is it? *(He shakes his head.)* Maybe in a hospital we'll be left alone. Given the lack of nurses, we probably will be left alone. *(moving towards the door)* It's going to be perfect.

MICHEL	Perfect.

They enter the living room.

CAROLYN	Hi everyone. You won't believe it. Michel and I just got married!
JANE	I thought something was going on.
DAWN	Congratulations.
JANE	How romantic. Just the two of you.
MICHEL	Three, with my mother.
JANE	Your mother was there?
MICHEL	On the phone.
CAROLYN	And I had Nana Bingham's wedding dress and Grampa's Bible. *(to JANE)* Are you angry?
JANE	It's not what I imagined but... your father and I love you and—
BILL	No. You're going to the hospital.
JANE	Bill.
CAROLYN	Daddy, it's all right.
BILL	Life is not a romantic picnic, Carolyn, and I will not stand around letting you make a fool of us.
CAROLYN	I'm not—
BILL	Put this coat around you.
CAROLYN	No!
BILL	You get in the car young lady.
MICHEL	You stay where you are.
BILL	Are you threatening me?
MICHEL	Oh yeah.
CAROLYN	*(steely and calm again)* It's all right Mish. Father and I are going to have a talk.
BILL	There's nothing to talk about.

CAROLYN	We're going to talk about the hospital.
BILL	Good.
CAROLYN	Alone. *(pointing to the bedroom)* In here.
BILL	Fine.

BILL manoeuvres past MICHEL and exits into the bedroom. CAROLYN follows.

DAWN	Wow. You guys are really getting a lot of stuff out.
JANE	We're not always like this.
RUSSELL	Because we're not always together.
JANE	Cause when we're together…

They look at each other.

| JANE & RUSSELL | …we're always like this. |

Scene Five – Father and Daughter

In the downstairs bedroom, CAROLYN is sitting on the bed. Her father hovers by the door.

CAROLYN	Sit down.
BILL	I'll stand.
CAROLYN	Then I'll stand too.

She struggles to stand.

BILL	All right. I'll sit.
CAROLYN	We'll sit together. And have a chat. A long overdue chat.
BILL	I'm listening.
CAROLYN	Number one. I will decide where I have my baby.
BILL	If you have your baby here you're a fool.

CAROLYN	Number two. I will not have you calling me a fool.
BILL	Then stop acting like one.
CAROLYN	(*furious*) Don't tell me what to do. I won't have it. Never again. Never, ever again.
	Pause.
	This is so not good for the baby.
BILL	That's right, and even if I weren't your father I am a doctor and—
CAROLYN	Stop. I don't want the doctor here. I want my father. Can you just be that? Can you just be my father?
BILL	I thought that's what I was doing.
CAROLYN	No. You have been the authority, the surgeon general, the CEO all evening, and all my life. Right now, I just want my dad.
BILL	Your dad is very worried.
CAROLYN	That's okay. Worrying is okay. Ordering me into your car is not okay.
BILL	It's hard. I think you're being very stubborn.
CAROLYN	Yes I am. I want what's best for my baby.
BILL	You're being irrational, Carolyn. A hospital birth is safer.
CAROLYN	You mean in case something goes wrong?
BILL	Exactly.
CAROLYN	I've had expert medical advice and I think things are going to go right. In fact, I know they're going to go right. And if they go wrong, then we can go to your hospital.
BILL	It's not my hospital.
CAROLYN	Okay, "the" hospital.
BILL	Why do you hate hospitals?

CAROLYN   I don't. Hospitals are great. But they're for sick people.
            I'm not sick. I don't want to be rushed through my
            labour. I don't want a C-section. I want to be in
            control.

BILL   Ha!

CAROLYN   There.

BILL   What?

CAROLYN   That's the sound Grampa makes when he's disgusted
            with something. Are you disgusted with me?

BILL   No.

CAROLYN   Ha!

BILL   It's just you're so difficult, Carolyn. Right from the start
            the simplest things become these horrible battles.

CAROLYN   So it's all my fault.

BILL   No but…

CAROLYN   (beat) Go on. Say it. (beat) We have to start talking,
            Daddy. We have to stop lying because we think it's
            kinder.

BILL   I remember taking you on my rounds of the maternity
            ward when you were a little girl. It was my first
            hospital. "Let's go and see the babies," I said. What
            a perfect place for a little girl who loved playing with
            dolls. Do you remember what happened?

CAROLYN   I didn't like it.

BILL   You ran screaming down the hall, smashed through
            a fire exit and set off the fire alarm, which forced an
            evacuation of the entire hospital. Three hundred
            patients carried out onto the front lawn, holding up
            their own I.V.'s because my daughter panicked looking
            at a nursing mother.

CAROLYN   I didn't know that.

BILL   I was disciplined by the hospital administration and for
            good reason. If it had been winter or raining, someone
            could have died.

CAROLYN	So you never took me there again.
BILL	Can you blame me?
CAROLYN	Never took me anywhere again.
BILL	I took you lots of places.
CAROLYN	With mummy. Never alone.
BILL	There were times.
CAROLYN	You took Joyce and Troy but never me. We were never alone again. *(realizing)* Until right now. I must have really hurt you, Daddy. You loved the hospital so much. You must have been so proud that day bringing your daughter for all the nurses to admire. And I hated it. All the red, scrunched up faces of the babies in their plastic boxes and the pale, sick women with tubes running out of their mouths and arms… I thought it was a death house. A monster house. And I ran and ran and all I ever wanted you to do was comfort me. I was just a little girl and I was frightened and all I wanted my father to do was to comfort me. Why couldn't you do that, Daddy?
BILL	I'm sorry.
CAROLYN	You're just saying that.
BILL	No, it's true. I was so humiliated, I never thought of you.
CAROLYN	Never loved me again.
BILL	Of course I loved you.
CAROLYN	No.
BILL	Oh Carolyn, please don't say that.
CAROLYN	You're lying. You're saying that because you think it's what I want to hear. I want you to say something real.
BILL	I'm not lying, Carolyn. I love you. I've always loved you. Loved you so much.
CAROLYN	Really?

CAROLYN's labour starts.

BILL	Oh honey, don't cry. Please don't cry.
CAROLYN	I'm not crying. Aaaaaah… Michel! The baby!

> *Some lively music is played which covers the following. MICHEL, DAWN and RUSSELL are already moving towards the room. They go through a rehearsed sequence of events that show they are totally prepared for the birth. Their equipment might include a plastic sheet on the bed, old sheets on top of that, receiving blankets, medical wipes, old towels, a bowl for the placenta, ice chips, and soothing music. MICHEL might try to set up a video camera only to be shooed away by DAWN. The tone should be playful in contrast to the emotions of the previous scene. BILL is dispatched for DAWN's bags. JANE and RUSSELL soon find themselves getting in the way and move out to the kitchen table. The door closes. The light in the bedroom is now very low.*

Scene Six – Waiting

RUSSELL	Are you all right, Janey?
JANE	(*weeping*) What? Yes. I'm fine.
RUSSELL	Everything's going to work out.
JANE	I hope so.
RUSSELL	You know I've never thanked you.
JANE	Thanked me? Thanked me for what?
RUSSELL	For marrying Bill. For taking him on.
JANE	Marrying Bill was the easiest thing I've ever done. He was such a brilliant young man.
RUSSELL	I guess I never saw that in him.
JANE	Everyone else did, Russell.
RUSSELL	Tell him, I think he did well.

JANE	Why don't you tell him yourself?
RUSSELL	I won't be here.
JANE	Where are you going?
RUSSELL	I'm crossing the bar.
JANE	The bar?
RUSSELL	The great divide.
JANE	Would you like a piece of pie before you go?
RUSSELL	No thanks. I've had enough to last a lifetime.

CAROLYN, supported by MICHEL and DAWN, crosses to use the bathroom. RUSSELL uses this distraction to exit outside.

CAROLYN	Hi Mum.
JANE	Are you all right?
CAROLYN	Oh yeah.
JANE	Can I help with anything?
CAROLYN	No, no. Just wanted to visit the powder room. Freshen up. Have a pee. Pull the duck.

MICHEL and CAROLYN continue and exit to the bathroom.

BILL enters with one of DAWN's bags.

DAWN	Thank you.
BILL	How was her blood pressure?
DAWN	122 on 70.
BILL	Foetal heart rate?
DAWN	135. Mother and child are doing fine.
BILL	Very good. *(He paces.)* I've never delivered in a domestic situation. I suppose it's normal to you.
DAWN	I've caught babies in kitchens, in cars, in bathtubs... I had a woman once, an Old Order Mennonite, fifth pregnancy, and she just *had* to milk her last three cows.

I had a feeling something was going to happen so
I followed her out with just a clamp and some scissors
and sure enough her waters broke and the baby came
right there in the straw.

BILL And you're confident about this one?

DAWN I have no reason not to be. Particularly now. How did
you get her labour started?

BILL Medically speaking, I did nothing. However in our
conversation I observed the mother experiencing
a strong emotional catharsis which may have caused
her uterus to relax and the labour to resume.

DAWN She had a good cry.

BILL Yes.

DAWN Tears are such a good sign.

BILL You look for signs?

DAWN Just ordinary things like vomiting or hiccups.

BILL What are hiccups a sign of?

DAWN Too much Guinness. I'm joking. Hiccups usually signal
the beginning of transition.

BILL Hmmm.

DAWN Doctor, when I attend births, I normally have one
or two women who assist me. I could call them, but
frankly I don't think they'd get here in time. I was
wondering, in an emergency, if you would assist me.

BILL You want *me* to assist *you*?

DAWN Only if necessary.

BILL I thought you were prepared for anything.

DAWN I am. But Carolyn's baby is big and coming fast. My
mothers very, very rarely have tears but if there is one,
I'm not very proud of my sutures.

BILL What kind do you use?

DAWN Intermittent.

BILL	Hmm. Can I teach you a little trick?
DAWN	Sure.
BILL	Come over here. *(They cross to the turkey.)* Let's pretend this bulge, where the stuffing is, is the perineum. Now—
	He stops speaking as CAROLYN and MICHEL re-enter and cross towards the bedroom.
CAROLYN	Hello. Here I am again. *(hic)* False alarm on the pee front, but I did manage to throw up. *(hic)* Mum, did you get the pie out of the oven?
JANE	Yes.
CAROLYN	Can you put the turkey back in?
JANE	Of course.
CAROLYN	Thanks. I can't believe you guys are here for this. Phew. Hard to walk.
	Both JANE and DAWN move forward to help. CAROLYN reaches for DAWN.
	It's okay, Mum. I got the team. See you later. *(hic)*
	They exit.
JANE	What are we doing here?
	She takes the pie out of the oven.
	She doesn't need me.
	She puts the turkey into the oven.
	We should go.
BILL	We can't leave now. She's just about to enter transition.
JANE	How do you know that? She's still walking around.
BILL	Hiccups. It's a sign.
JANE	I've just been thinking about all the dreams I had for her. The wedding, and the baptism, and the baby's first Royal Doulton figurine... which I've already bought. Tell me I'm not ridiculous.

BILL	You, personally, raised two and a half million dollars for the new birthing ward.
JANE	Yes I did.
BILL	When they saw you coming, the captains of industry threw up their hands and took out their chequebooks.
JANE	Only the ones I dated in high school. Bill, do you think we held on too long?
BILL	To Carolyn?
JANE	To all of them.
BILL	Probably. But it's hard to stand back when your children are being as stupid as you were.
JANE	Excuse me? My children are not stupid. We were not stupid.
BILL	Well...
JANE	Honestly, Bill, where do you get these ideas?
BILL	*(with difficulty)* I just wanted my children to turn out better than I did, so the world would be better than it is... and instead, thank God, they ended up being themselves.
JANE	You never told me that before.
BILL	The last time we talked was on our honeymoon.
JANE	Stop.
BILL	Because right after that you got pregnant.
JANE	Because I'd been waiting half a lifetime for you to graduate.
BILL	Well, waiting gave us lots of opportunity to practice.
JANE	That's true.
BILL	The intern's lounge.
JANE	The ambulance.
BILL & JANE	The morgue.

JANE	My gosh, Bill. Hasn't it gone fast?
BILL	Are you kidding? It's been kids for thirty years.
JANE	And now there's just us.
BILL	Just us.

Pause.

What a relief.

JANE	No kidding.
BILL	No more pager.
JANE	Let's leave right now.
BILL	And do what?
JANE	I dunno. Empty your wine cellar.
BILL	You don't want to stay?
JANE	She's forgotten I'm here. Do you really need to stay?
BILL	The midwife did ask me to assist.
JANE	We could wait in the car.
BILL	And do what?
JANE	Something we might regret.

DAWN enters.

DAWN	Mrs. Bingham, we're just about to start pushing. Carolyn would like you to come in.
JANE	Me?
DAWN	Yes.
BILL	Well…
JANE	Tell her I'll be right in.

DAWN exits.

BILL	What are you waiting for?
JANE	I was enjoying sitting here with you.
BILL	I'm not going anywhere.

JANE	I know. But do you think we're going to be all right?
BILL	I want to be.
JANE	I don't want to end up just going through the motions.
BILL	We won't.
JANE	How do you know?
BILL	I don't but I sensed that was what you wanted me to say.
JANE	You're such a jerk. Don't go away.
BILL	I won't.
JANE	How's my lipstick?
BILL	Perfect.
JANE	*(turning at the door)* Oh Bill, isn't this wonderful. Our daughter's having a baby!
BILL	So get in there.
JANE	Thank you, thank you, thank you, thank you.
DAWN	Okay, Carolyn. You can start pushing.
	Composing herself, she exits.
BILL	Well, I can tell you one thing. This would never have happened in a hospital. *(He looks around.)* Dad?
	We hear CAROLYN's labour and the encouragement of her team.
	(calling softly out the stage left door) Dad?
DAWN	Okay, Carolyn. You can start pushing.
	BILL grabs his coat and exits outside.

Scene Seven – Birth and Death

> *CAROLYN's labour continues as RUSSELL enters*
> *downstage right and sits on his wood-splitting stump.*

RUSSELL   First you get cold. Then you go numb. Then you go
to sleep and the polar bears come. Saves on the burial.
I guess they'll have to store me somewhere 'till the
ground thaws. (*He thinks.*) Well, they'll figure it out.
But the thing is, I'll be out of her way... and she'll have
the babe.

Holy jumpin', it's cold.

Lorna? I got the recipe right. Carolyn and I worked
at it and we got it right. God I love to see work done.
I love doing it, planning it, talking about it. I was good
at working and you were good at everything else.
Birthdays, feast days, holidays. You kept all our
memories. Keep a light in the window, I won't be long.

> *We hear CAROLYN groan.*

DAWN   The baby's head is there, Carolyn. You can feel the
baby's head.

CAROLYN   It hurts.

MICHEL   You're doing great.

JANE   You're doing beautifully darling.

DAWN   C'mon, another push.

> *CAROLYN strains.*

RUSSELL   First you get cold. Then you go numb. Lord, I love the
way light sparkles on snow. (*He sees salvation.*) Oh
Lord.... Oh sweet mercy.

> *RUSSELL's head falls gently on his chest.*
>
> *We hear the final moments of the birth.*

MICHEL   Come on... you're almost there...

JANE   Keep going... just a little more...

DAWN	Push Carolyn, push…
	These voices, with CAROLYN's, reach a climax and then stop. A baby's cry.
MICHEL	*(softly)* It's a girl. A little girl.
JANE	Oh Carolyn…
DAWN	Good colour. Nice weight. Lots of hair.
CAROLYN	Let me see. Let me see.
DAWN	Here's your baby, Carolyn.
	DAWN moves the child to CAROLYN's chest.
CAROLYN	Oh. Hello little one.
BILL	*(off)* Dad?
	BILL enters down left. He sees RUSSELL collapsed against the woodpile.
	Ohmigod. Dad? Dad? Dad. I'm taking you inside.
	BILL embraces RUSSELL…
RUSSELL	Lorna?
	…and then lifts him.
	(waking) What the hell's going on.
	Dropping him.
BILL	Dad. Are you all right?
RUSSELL	Of course I'm all right.
BILL	Take a pill.
RUSSELL	I don't need a pill. What's the matter with you?
BILL	You disappeared from the house. I didn't know where you'd gone.
RUSSELL	Do I need permission to get some fresh air? Why are you limping?
BILL	I hurt my back.
RUSSELL	Sweet jumpin' jehosophat, you are a piece of work.

BILL	Me?! I thought you were dead. I thought you'd come out here to die.
RUSSELL	Now why would I do a thing like that? And with Carolyn having her baby?
BILL	I thought that's *why* you wanted to do it. Because Carolyn's going to have a baby and you didn't want to be a burden.
RUSSELL	I've been a burden to women all my life. Why should it bother me now?
BILL	Then why have you been talking about dying?
RUSSELL	You're shivering.
BILL	It's cold out here.
RUSSELL	Take my coat.
BILL	I'm not going to take your coat.
RUSSELL	I'm used to the cold, you're not.

BILL sits. RUSSELL drapes the coat over both of them.

	That's what your mother used to say when you were up with your books and I wanted you to do farm work. She'd say, "Leave him alone. He's not used to it."
BILL	But you didn't leave me alone, did you?
RUSSELL	My dad made me work. Why should you get a free ride?
BILL	I didn't get a free ride.
RUSSELL	Ha!
BILL	I worked hard and I did well. Something you don't seem to have noticed.
RUSSELL	I noticed.
BILL	Ha!
RUSSELL	I had a cow step on my big toe the other month. Swole up so bad I couldn't get my boot off. The young doctor in town—Murray Jenkin's son.

BILL	Arthur.
RUSSELL	Yeah. Arthur. Looks like he's straight outta high school. He says you're the best man for babies in the province. He says you wrote the book on babies.
BILL	And what did you say?
RUSSELL	I can't remember. *(BILL sighs.)* At that moment he was lifting off my toenail. But later… it struck me that maybe I hadn't mentioned that I thought you'd done pretty well in your life even if you couldn't do a single day in the barn.
BILL	What are you trying to say, Dad?
RUSSELL	I just said what I'm trying to say.
BILL	Are you trying to say you're proud of me?
RUSSELL	Why would I say a thing like that?
BILL	Presumably, because you think it's true.
RUSSELL	It is true.
BILL	Then why don't you say it?
RUSSELL	That's your mother's job.
BILL	Mum's not here.
RUSSELL	So. When you get to where she is, she can tell you.
BILL	I'd like to hear you say it. Now. Unless it's too much work.
RUSSELL	I can say it easy enough. I'm right proud of you. Your mum and I both. We're just right proud of you.
BILL	Thanks Dad.
RUSSELL	There's more of me in you than I thought. Do you want to go in?
BILL	We should, shouldn't we?

> *They sit in companionable silence.*

I had this husband and wife show up at the hospital last week. Nice couple. Mother was a little anaemic

but nothing serious and we had a very normal delivery
except the baby didn't breathe. I did everything
I could, but the baby just wouldn't breathe. Died
in my hands. I still don't know why. Could've done
a Caesarean I guess. I don't think that it would have
made any difference but it might have. Maybe all
babies should be delivered by caesarean. Anyway, just
so you know, I'm resigning my position at the hospital.
They want me to stay, which is nice, but I think it's
time to do a little teaching... a little research.

RUSSELL   Sleep through the night.

*Their attention is distracted by noises inside the
house. MICHEL is opening a bottle of champagne.*

BILL   Sounds like there's a baby.

RUSSELL   I can see it now. The Frenchman, weeping, overcome
with the glory of it all. Actually, this'd be a good time
to go look at his barn.

BILL   Dad. I'm cold.

RUSSELL   It's warm in the barn. We can do some work. Milk the
cows.

BILL   I never liked being in the barn with you.

RUSSELL   I know. It was disappointing. For both of us. But things
have changed. You'd like it now.

BILL   I swore I would never go in there again.

RUSSELL   Well, I can always stay out here alone. *(He coughs.)*

BILL   All right. But I'm not working.

RUSSELL   Oh, you won't hardly have to. There's tubes and pumps
and buttons. I get to push the buttons.

BILL   You know how to operate all this?

RUSSELL   Oh my yes. But we should be quiet. Out of respect for
the new child.

_____ Denouement

> *As they exit, lights come up on MICHEL holding the baby. He's snoring. Time has passed. CAROLYN is comfortably ensconced in RUSSELL's chair. DAWN is leaving.*

JANE   I wish you'd have something to eat.

DAWN   There will be food where I'm going.

JANE   I can't believe you're going to attend another birth.

DAWN   This one will be simpler.

JANE   How do you know?

DAWN   Her parents live in Vancouver. *(to CAROLYN)* I'll drop by in a couple of days.

CAROLYN   Thanks for everything.

DAWN   Don't thank me. You were magnificent.

> *She leaves.*

JANE   She's right. You were courageous and strong.

> *CAROLYN indicates she wants more.*

And beautiful and vulnerable and very generous to let your mother be a part of it.

CAROLYN   It was nice to have you there.

JANE   I had no idea how dramatic it all is.

CAROLYN   C'mon. You had three babies.

JANE   Oh, I was conked out. I wanted to be.

CAROLYN   Wasn't Daddy there?

JANE   Goodness no.

CAROLYN   Why not?

JANE   I didn't want him there. I didn't want him to see me like that.

CAROLYN   You mean, conked out?

JANE	No, without make-up.
CAROLYN	Ow. Don't make me laugh.
JANE	But you know… seeing you and Michel so close… I was a little jealous.
CAROLYN	He was great.
JANE	Carolyn. May I visit sometimes?
CAROLYN	How often is sometimes?
JANE	Once a week. I could help with the baby.
CAROLYN	Let's take it slow.
JANE	But we can at least go shopping for baby clothes, right?
CAROLYN	Sure.
JANE	I'll pick you up tomorrow.

CAROLYN laughs and groans. BILL and RUSSELL enter.

BILL	Hello.
JANE	Where have you two been?
BILL	In the barn.
MICHEL	*(waking)* The barn? Who was in the barn?
BILL	Relax. It's all done.
MICHEL	What's done?
RUSSELL	The wood.
BILL	The cows. All 72 of them. Dad knew the whole drill.
MICHEL	He did?
RUSSELL	Ain't hardly work anymore.
BILL	Can I see the baby?

MICHEL passes the baby to BILL.

JANE	It's a girl.
CAROLYN	Ten toes, ten fingers, two ears, one nose.

BILL	Perfect.
JANE	Carolyn was fabulous.
BILL	Look, Dad.
RUSSELL	Oh my…
BILL	She's got Mum's eyes, doesn't she?
RUSSELL	I saw that right off.

The phone rings.

MICHEL	That'll be my mother.
JANE	Is anyone hungry? The turkey must be cooked by now.
CAROLYN	Finally.
MICHEL	*Allo maman.*
BILL	I'm hungry.
JANE	I'll bring you a plate.

The lights begin to fade.

MICHEL   *Oui, oui, la bébé est arrivé et elle est belle comme un coeur. Cheveux noirs, yeux bruns, deux bras, deux jambs, dix doights. // Bien oui. Elle s'appelle Hope, Mama. La bébé s'appelle Hope.*

The end.

David S. Craig is one of Canada's most prolific and influential dramatists for youth and family audiences. He has written more than twenty professionally produced plays including *Having Hope at Home* and *Fires in the Night* for the Blyth Festival, *Booster McCrane, P.M.* for Toronto Free Theatre and *Cue for Treason,* for Young Peoples Theatre. His one-man show *Napalm the Magnificent* won the Chalmers New Play Award and his performance was nominated for a Dora Mavor Moore Award. David has created the internationally acclaimed *Danny, King of the Basement* for Roseneath Theatre which has been seen extensively across Canada, the United States, the United Kingdom, Germany and Austria, and *Smokescreen,* which examines adolescent marijuana use. David has extensive writing credits in radio drama having created a fifty-one part series based on *Booster Crane, P.M.* for Morningside, a fifty episode series called *The Diamond Lane* for Metro Morning, and the award-winning ninety-minute Christmas Special, *The First Christmas. NOW* magazine named David S. Craig, "one of the top twenty playwrights in Canada." Mr. Craig is currently the Artistic Director of Roseneath Theatre (www.roseneath.ca).